MOTHBALLS
& ELBOW GREASE

Origins and meanings
of household sayings

National Trust

First published in the United Kingdom in 2002
This edition published in 2011 by
National Trust Books
10 Southcombe Street
London W14 0RA

An imprint of Anova Books Company Ltd

Packaged by Susanna Geoghegan

ISBN: 9781907892165

A CIP catalogue record for this book is
available from the British Library.

17 16 15 14 13 12 11
10 9 8 7 6 5 4 3 2 1

Typeset by seagulls.net
Printed in China by Kwong Fat

This book can be ordered direct from the publisher at the
website www.anovabooks.com, or try your local bookshop.
Also available at National Trust shops and
www.nationaltrustbooks.co.uk.

Contents

Introduction

The English penchant for wordplay is, perhaps, nowhere more evident than in the staggering array of metaphors, similes and catchphrases with which we furnish everyday speech. Far from calling a spade a spade, over the centuries we have devised an elaborate phraseology to embellish the litany of life.

We use the familiar to describe the novel. We qualify emotions and justify actions by drawing parallels between seemingly unconnected events or items. We dilute the absurdities and tragedies of everyday existence with euphemism, and we abbreviate explanation by use of time-honoured expressions.

The well from which we draw inspiration is deep. Historical events, the church, the countryside, industry, sport, government and the military have all provided countless everyday sayings. But if you want to explore the connections between the social history of Britain and language, the home is where you need to begin.

It is hard to imagine, in these days of international travel and satellite communication, that for centuries the scope of life for the majority of people was, comparatively, minute. Home was not only where the heart was but also the body of life itself. The mechanics of living took up an inordinate amount of time and energy and the tools of domesticity were often cumbersome and inefficient compared to their modern equivalents. Such restraints meant that the focus of life was housebound. Domestic chores and household items had a significance that was woven into the fabric of everyday life and speech.

A great number of the expressions that have survived into the twenty-first century have done so because either they remain pertinent or because centuries of use has imbued them with a relevance we still understand. We all know that a 'watched pot never boils'; and the development of electricity has done little to diminish the potentially disastrous consequences of having 'too many irons in the fire'.

Other sayings have been lost to modern speech because we no longer recognise the reference or allusion. The dictates of fashion alone have made many expressions obsolete. People still 'stand upon their pantables' but if you accused someone of doing so today, no doubt they would look at you blankly.

Mothballs and Elbow Grease contains sayings, proverbs and catchphrases that fall into all three categories and also explores the origin of some everyday items. In all, these explanations provide an illuminating insight into domestic life over the ages. Not only do they illustrate the verbal ingenuity of our ancestors, but they also show how much common phraseology is indebted to the commonplace.

The Kitchen

Through the centuries, phrases about food and its preparation have provided a fascinating insight into the development of the kitchen.

From time immemorial, cooking in small houses was done over an open hearth in the communal living area. Individual kitchens, with built-in ovens, developed in larger houses in the early Middle Ages, but were usually detached due to fire risk. The seventeenth century brought unprecedented architectural experimentation. Formal mansions became fashionable, with symmetrically arranged rooms and a vertical hierarchy of space, resulting in the kitchen being relocated in the basement. Although the basement kitchen remained commonplace, around a hundred years later in large, classically influenced houses the kitchen and attendant rooms were often positioned in a side wing, distancing the noise and odour, and increasing the sense of separation from the servants. The opportunity and desire to amalgamate the kitchen and service functions into one room incorporated within the main body of the house did not come about until well into the twentieth century. Often handed down from generation to generation, the many food-related expressions reflect our rich culinary history.

A lid to match the kettle

To ensure that a kettle is as efficient as possible it needs a tight-fitting lid, and this is the reference when it is said of a married couple that 'the lid matches the kettle'. It means that they are very well suited.

A watched pot never boils

This is a concise way of suggesting that impatience and anxiety will not make things happen any faster. In the days when cooks needed to rely on the vagaries of an open fire and solid fuel, there must have been many a 'watched pot'. But even today, when cooking is a far more regulated science, the pressures of life mean the expression is commonly understood as a mild reproof to someone who is overly impatient for a particular outcome.

All smoked gammon and pickles

This delicious-sounding phrase was used to describe anything that was all 'stuff and nonsense'. Gammon was initially thieves' slang for a hoax or deceit, used in such expressions as 'to keep in gammon' – which meant to engage a person's attention while an accomplice was robbing him. An alternative to the 'pickles' element of the expression was 'spinach'.

Apple-pie order

The origin of this expression is dubious but it is generally agreed that it has nothing whatsoever to do with apples, cooking or even the kitchen. It is used to convey the idea that everything is in its right place, neat and ordered. Some suggest that it comes from the French, *cap à pied*, which is a military description of a knight in full armour – one armed from head to foot. Others favour the idea that the expression derives from another French term, *nappe pliée*, a folded tablecloth or sheet. Both French terms convey the idea of order and neatness necessary to anything being in 'apple-pie order'.

Apron-husband

A man who meddled in his wife's work would be dubbed an 'apron-husband'. But it was also said that 'the cunning wife makes her husband her apron', which meant that it was sensible to get one's spouse to perform all the dirtiest duties of a household.

Argue the leg off an iron pot

The absurdity of the notion only goes to emphasise how argumentative you would need to be to have this expression hurled at you. Another saying with the same meaning was to 'argue off a dog's tail' – an equally ridiculous proposition.

As cool as a cucumber

The humble cucumber was already being grown in England in the sixteenth century but enjoyed a far from enviable reputation. Cucumbers were thought to have a dampening effect on lust, and the first version of the simile, 'as cold as a cucumber', was applied particularly to women. In 1732, the playwright John Gay referred to 'as cool as a cucumber' as 'a new simile' and it eventually took over from the original expression. It is used to describe someone who is composed and self-possessed.

Curiously, 'cucumber' was also a slang name for a tailor, and 'cucumber-time' was from mid-July to mid-September (the cucumber growing season), when traditionally tailors' workshops were quiet and when tailors had leave to play.

As sure as eggs is eggs

Ungrammatical though it may be, this expression is a long-winded way of saying something is a certainty. It has been suggested that the original expression was the algebraic formula 'X is X', and that, in common use, it was transformed by those whose mathematical knowledge was poor.

Bread and cheese

This term is used to denote the barest necessities of life, while something that is described as being 'bread and cheese' is ordinary or commonplace. Certainly, bread has been a staple part of our diet since very early times, although originally the word 'bread' in Old English meant simply a piece or fragment. Bread, as we know it, was called 'loaf' and it was not until the early thirteenth century that the words took on the meaning we understand today, with 'bread' being the substance and 'loaf' an individual article thereof. There is no positive evidence of cheese being made in Britain before the Romans, who were adept in separating milk curd and allowing it to sour either naturally or by the addition of various vegetable extracts, and then pressing it into a mass. Soon however, cheese was being made in dairies and farmhouses across the land and it became an essential part of daily life, but it was not until 1870 that the first English cheese factory was established.

Bread basket

In the sixteenth century a bread basket was just what it says it was, a basket for holding or handing round bread, but two hundred years later it became a street fighter's term for 'stomach'. The idea then progressed into the stomach also being referred to as the 'bread room', 'dumpling-depot', and even the 'porridge bowl'. Such terms were used particularly when someone was punched or kicked in that part of his anatomy.

Bread never falls but on its buttered side

This proverb, expressing how misfortune can be complete, first put in an appearance in the nineteenth century and is a forerunner of what many people consider today as Murphy's, or Sod's, Law.

Captain Edward A. Murphy was an American engineer, who, while working on a particular project in 1949, came to the conclusion that 'if anything can go wrong, it will'. The project manager kept a list of such sayings and scribbled down the quote, which he called Murphy's Law.

Cheese-paring policy

Any cost-saving policy that is deemed to be excessively stingy or drastic could be described as 'cheese-paring'. The reference is to actions of an excessively economical person who pares the rind of a cheese carefully and closely to ensure the least possible waste.

Cook one's goose

The first time this expression appeared in print was around 1850 and it is thought to have been a line in a popular play in which one of the characters decides that to save his own 'bacon' he must, in turn, cook another's goose. It means to bring about the ruin or downfall of another – or oneself, in the case of cooking one's own goose. There is no reliable evidence to explain why a goose is the chosen bird or, indeed, why cooking it should be so significant. It may possibly refer to a goose being fattened for the table where it is due to take pride of place on a special occasion, that is eaten prematurely, leaving nothing for the event for which it is has been designated.

Cupboard love

A show of love based on self-interest or the prospect of gain is called 'cupboard love'. It is thought to stem from the childish practice of lavishing affection on any indulgent person who provides tasty morsels or treats from the store. In the early nineteenth century it was commonly understood that 'cupboard love is seldom true'. As for cupboards – a cupboard was originally just what it says it was – an open board or plank on which to store cups and plates. By 1530 it had taken on the meaning of being 'a closet or cabinet with shelves for keeping cups, dishes, provisions etc' and had moved out of the kitchen. Henry VIII had a cupboard of twelve shelves for displaying his gold ware, the number of shelves one could display being determined by one's status. It is noted in *The Life of Cardinal Wolsey*, by George Cavendish, that the proud man boasted a 'Cup Borde … six desks [shelves] high'. Dukes, on the other hand, were permitted only four or five, lesser noblemen three, and the mere gentleman only one.

Cup tosser

Far from being a servant adept at moving china from one place to another, a cup tosser was a juggler. The original symbol for a juggler was a goblet, or cup, in recognition of the tricks the artist could perform with such an article.

Do not go to the devil with a dishclout in your hand

The more commonly known expression that conveys the same sentiment is the old proverb 'one might as well be hanged for a sheep as a lamb'. The idea is that if you are going to do something dishonest or disreputable you might as well get as much out of it as you can.

Eggs on the spit

The full expression is 'I have eggs on the spit' and it means that you are very busy indeed and have no time for other matters. The reference is to an old, time-consuming recipe and the 'spit' is a toasting fork, rather than the conventional spit we think of for roasting meat. To roast an egg is not as impossible as it sounds. First you boil your egg, peel it and remove the yolk. That you mix with a variety of spices and then replace the mixture into the egg, before carefully threading the stuffed egg onto a toasting fork and holding it over the fire. Such a delicate concoction required close attention or the dish would be ruined.

Fire dogs

Now a common term for andirons in a fireplace, fire dogs were once real animals caged in a wheel at one end of a roasting spit. The dogs would run round the wheel, in turn spinning the spit. Doctor John Caius (who in 1557 refounded and extended Gonville and Caius College, Cambridge) once noted: 'There is comprehended under the curs of the coarsest kind a certain dog in kitchen service excellent. For when any meat is to be roasted, they go into a wheel, which they turning about with the weight of their bodies, so diligently look to their business, that no drudge or scullion can do the meat more cunningly, whom the popular sort hereupon term turnspits.'

It was said then, and still is, that meat so perfectly cooked was 'done to a turn'.

Flummery

In its literal sense, 'flummery' was a pudding made of boiled oatmeal that, while tasty, was not over-nourishing. In its figurative use, 'flummery' is flattery or empty compliments.

Fry in one's own grease

To suffer the consequences of your own folly is to 'fry in your own grease'. Another culinary version of the sentiment is 'stew in your own juice'. Both expressions have been common for centuries. Chaucer used the 'fry' version in the prologue to the *Wife of Bath's Tale*: 'In his own gress I made him frie, For anger and for verry jalousie.'

Gander month

As well as being a male goose, 'gander' was a slang term for a married man and one suspects there may be many a 'gander' today who would appreciate the opportunity to enjoy a 'gander month'. Traditionally it was the four weeks after a woman had given birth, when it was held excusable for her husband to play away from home. Any man who made the most of his chances was called a 'gander-mooner'.

Gentleman who pays the rent

The importance of the cottage pig is emphasised in this expression. For many families, the pig was the greatest asset they owned and provided not only food for themselves but also the wherewithal to trade and to barter. It was said that you could use every part of a pig except its squeak, and there are numerous old recipes that support the claim.

Going to pot

This expression, meaning to be ruined or destroyed, does little to flatter culinary art. It refers to meat or vegetables being chopped up into small enough pieces to be thrown into the ubiquitous cooking pot, the implication being that the value of it is lost forever. It is thought to be a shorter version of the expression 'go to the pot' which was known to be in use in the mid-sixteenth century.

Half a loaf is better than no bread

This admonition to be content with one's lot was first recorded in John Heywood's *Dialogue of Proverbs* in 1546: 'Throwe no gyft agayne at the giuers head, For better is halfe a lofe then no bread.' It plainly means that something is better than nothing.

In the same oven

In common parlance, to be 'in the same oven' was to be in the same plight. The expression neatly conveyed the idea of being in a hot and uncomfortable position.

It boils down to

Any cook will tell you that to increase the potency of a good bone stock to make a glaze, it needs to be 'reduced', by boiling off a large percentage of the water content.

What is left is flavoursome concentrate that can be added to a variety of dishes. Figuratively, 'to boil something down' is to get to the heart of the matter, the essential factor of any situation.

Jug-handled

Jugs commonly have only one handle and it is this simple fact that has led to the term 'jug-handled' being used to describe an argument that is unbalanced or a contract that is too one-sided. The converse to this is the expression 'every pot has two handles': that is to say that there are two sides to every argument.

Know which side one's bread is buttered

For hundreds of years this term has been used to describe someone who is aware of where his best interests lie, even though butter was despised as a food by the upper and middle classes until the eighteenth century when it became popular as a spread for bread. (Prior to that butter was principally used as a medicine. It was made mainly in the spring and the summer and heavily salted to preserve it for future use. As a curious aside, butter made in May was considered particularly beneficial to children for the treatment of constipation and growing pains!)

Little pitchers have wide ears

This was used as a warning that it was unwise to say anything in front of children that you did not wish repeated. Common kitchen vessels for centuries, pitchers were traditionally large earthenware pots with a lip and two large ear-shaped handles.

Make a hash of something

The problem of how to turn leftovers from one meal into another has tested cooks for hundreds of years. In many instances, the easy answer was to prepare a 'hash' – a concoction of mixed up meat, vegetables, gravy and sauce. (The word comes from the Old French, *hacher*, to chop or to mince.) From the early eighteenth century the term has also been applied figuratively and means to make a mess or a jumble of something or a situation; to do something badly.

Mollycoddle

When used as a verb, 'to mollycoddle' means to indulge or pamper. Used as noun, it was a term for an effeminate man, as indeed was 'molly' on its own; and it is from that sense that the first part of the term is said to derive. The 'coddle' half is thought to relate to the culinary method of 'coddling', which is a gentle form of boiling or stewing. The word 'coddle' itself is thought to be a dialect version of 'caudle', which was a warm drink of thin spiced gruel mixed with wine or ale that was considered highly beneficial for invalids.

Neither fish nor fowl

Something that is neither one thing nor another and so is useless to all, is referred to as being 'neither fish nor fowl'. The full expression is 'neither fish, flesh (or fowl), nor good red herring'. The expression dates from the Middle Ages when specific foods were indicative of the various classes of society. Fish was food for the clergy, flesh (or fowl) was the sustenance of the common man, and red herrings were the fare of paupers.

Nutmeg grater

The nutmeg has been a favoured spice since Roman times, and is the highly aromatic seed of an evergreen tree that is indigenous to the East Indian islands. Any good cook will tell you that to get the best out of a nutmeg you should store it whole and grate a little each time you need it. Consequently small graters were designed for this particular purpose. Whether or not it was the shape of early nutmeg graters that gave rise to the term being used as a slang expression for a man's beard is unknown.

On the shelf

The age at which a woman resigns herself to being 'on the shelf', with no prospect of marriage, has changed dramatically over the centuries – but the allusion remains the same. The 'shelf' in the kitchen was where items not needed on a daily basis were put.

Out of the frying pan and into the fire

This expression has been common in England since the sixteenth century, but most languages have similar expressions for conveying the idea of getting out of one 'hot spot' directly into another, and have had for centuries. The early Greeks, for example, went 'out of the smoke and into the flame'.

Over-egg the pudding

The danger of putting too much of any ingredient into a dish is a 'recipe for disaster', and in the case of eggs it is no exception. In a non-literal sense, 'to over-egg the pudding' means to wildly exaggerate or overstate your case, which in a figurative sense could also be another 'recipe for disaster'.

Pantry

While now used to refer to a room used to store a variety of foodstuffs, originally a pantry was for the exclusive storage of bread. The word comes from the Old French, *paneterie*, a cupboard for keeping bread. In the great English country and town houses, there would be several pantries, the most important of which was the 'butler's pantry' where the plate for the table was kept under the watchful eye of the man who held the highest rank 'below stairs'.

Potluck

A much-used term to express the idea of random choice. The essential utensil in the medieval kitchen was a cast-iron cauldron in which all manner of 'pottage' could be created. This soup-like stew was part of the staple diet and at its most basic consisted of vegetables boiled in stock. In peasant households nearly everything that was edible would end up in the pot. In households where there was not a beam to hang a cauldron from, an earthenware pot would be balanced among the embers to serve the same purpose. Should a visitor be invited to join in a meal, he would be given the opportunity to dip into the pot, taking his chance that he would scoop up the choicest morsels.

Potboiler

This term refers to something that is done purely for the money it will earn, and is used mainly to describe the work of artists and writers where the commercial aspects outweigh the artistic or literary value of the product. It encapsulates the idea of providing an income to 'keep the pot boiling', which in turn means to keep interest alive in a project and things progressing apace.

Pot calling the kettle black

This is said of someone who accuses another of something of which he, himself, is guilty. Until the Industrial Revolution introduced new methods of producing steel, cooking pots were generally made from iron and were, by nature, black. The specific use of the word kettle to denote a covered vessel with a handle and a spout used principally for boiling water did not come about in Britain until the seventeenth century with the introduction of tea into Europe. It was not until the 1920s that aluminium (first commercially produced in 1886 in France and the USA) became the favoured metal for domestic cooking utensils. Nowadays, that prolific writer, *Anon*, suggests that the modern kitchen is where the pot calls the kettle chartreuse.

Randle tree

The iron bar that used to be placed across a chimney to hang pots and pans over a fire was called, in Scotland, a 'randle tree'. When the term was applied to a person it graphically explained succinctly that he was tall and thin.

Right as a trivet

The common metal three-legged stand for pots and pans can only stand upright. Any person considered to be equally upstanding was described as being as 'right as a trivet'.

Salt away

Before the mid-nineteenth century and the development of refrigeration, if you wanted to preserve food you needed to rely on time-tested methods: salting, spicing, smoking, pickling or drying. Salt was the most commonly used preservative, both in crystal form or diluted in water as brine. Therefore to 'salt' something away was to save it for future use. In time the expression came to be used with particular reference to money put aside for a 'rainy day'.

Saucepan lid

In rhyming slang, 'saucepan lid' was a 'quid' or a sovereign (latterly a pound). The word 'quid' is itself seventeenth-century slang and is thought to come from the Latin, *quid pro quo*, literally meaning 'something for something'.

Save one's bacon

There are two ideas about why this expression conveys the idea of saving oneself from injury or harm. The first is based on the importance of 'bacon' as the principal meat that was salted and preserved for the lean

winter months. Undoubtedly, the diligent housewife would take steps to prevent such a store being tampered with, or raided, to ensure her family was catered for until spring. However, the second explanation is based on the idea that the Anglo-Saxon word for 'back' was *baec*, which was also the Old Dutch word for 'bacon'. Therefore to 'save one's bacon', it is thought, was to literally save one's back from a thrashing.

Scrambled eggs

While the origin is definitely domestic, the term 'scrambled eggs' is Royal Air Force slang for the ornate gold oak leaves on the cap peak of any officer from Group Captain up, and especially an Air Commodore. When used in the singular, i.e. 'scrambled egg', it is used to describe the wearer rather than the cap.

Scrape the kettle

It was the job of the scullion to scrape the kettles and keep them clean and scum-free, and when used in a figurative sense it also implies the act of cleansing. Metaphorically speaking, to 'scrape the kettle' was to go to confession.

Scullery and scullion

The scullery was the room or department of a house where dishes, pots and kitchen utensils were washed and cared for. The word was in use in England by 1440 and comes from the Old French, *esculserie*, the maker or seller of dishes. The scullery was the domain of the 'scullion', the lowest ranking domestic servant. In medieval kitchens, scullions were young boys who lived in the kitchen and, more often than not, slept on its floor. They performed the most menial tasks and did not even enjoy free access to the other rooms in the kitchen complex. While now obsolete, by the seventeenth century the word 'scullion' had evolved into an abusive term for someone deemed to be base or mean.

Simper like a furmity-kettle

Furmity, or frumenty, was made of hulled wheat boiled in milk and seasoned with sugar and spices, and a 'furmity-kettle' was a particular vessel specifically designed for the making of this very popular dish. To 'simper like a furmity-kettle' was to be all smiles and to look merry. The allusion may be to the bubbling and cheerful appearance of the furmity while it is cooking, not to mention its sweet aroma.

Small potatoes

Anything that is insignificant or worth little can be described as 'small potatoes' and has been for a very long time. It is thought that the first potatoes were brought to England on board Sir Francis Drake's ship returning from the first Virginia colony in 1586. The vegetable is first mentioned in print in 1596 in a catalogue of the plants grown in a London garden. It was a crop much favoured by the poorer elements of society as it provided more per acre and demanded less attention than any other. However, it was not until the nineteenth century that the potato was established as a staple national food, even though it had been an essential part of the rural diet for more than a hundred years.

Square meal

There is no definite evidence to explain where this catchphrase originates. However, it has been suggested that it comes from the predecessors of an essential item of crockery. Long before plates as we know them were in common use, food was served on trenchers. These were made from square-cut slices of stale brown bread hollowed out in the centre. A wealthy man would have several trenchers for his use during a meal, the more humble only one or two. At the end of the meal the trenchers would be gathered up and given to the poor. In time, wood took over from bread. The new-look trencher was a square of wood, again with a large hollow in the centre but with the addition of a small hollow in one corner for salt. If plentiful, the food would be piled into the centre of the square thus providing a full and satisfying meal.

Take with a pinch of salt

This expression, which has been in common use since the mid-seventeenth century comes directly from the Latin *cum grano selis*. It is used to advise against wholly believing any extravagant or inaccurate claim. It suggests that taking a grain of salt with something will make it easier to swallow and more palatable.

Taking the gilt off the gingerbread

To counteract the dull, dark appearance of gingerbread, there was a time when ginger cakes were gilded with a thin layer of real gold leaf, or Dutch leaf – which looked like gold – to make them appear more appetising. These golden delights were popular fairground fare but once the gilt was removed the cake could be seen for what it really was. In time the expression became synonymous with showing something to be less valuable than initial appearances would suggest, or with destroying an illusion.

Tea caddy

The word comes from the Malay, *kati*, a weight of about one and a half pounds which came to be applied to a box of tea containing that amount. It originally came into English as *catty*, and for some unexplained reason in the eighteenth century took on its current spelling.

The cooks' own

Quite how this expression came into being is unknown, but in the nineteenth century 'The Cooks' Own' was a colloquialism for the Police Force. It has been suggested that it is a joke reference to the name of army regiments, linked to the popular Victorian conception that there was many a special relationship between the cook of a household and the local bobby.

The proof of the pudding is in the eating

The 'proof' in the context of this old proverb, means 'test' and considering that the expression was first recorded back in the fourteenth century and has remained unaltered ever since, it would seem to be as valid as what it implies. For just as eating a pudding is the only way to fully assess how good it really is, performance not appearance is the only way to judge a person's ability and talent – or even an expression's ability to encapsulate a basic truth.

To make larder of something or someone

This expression, meaning to slaughter or kill, comes from the idea of preparing meat for store. The word larder is now used to describe a storeroom for a variety of food and provisions but it comes from the Old French *lardoir*, which was specifically a storeroom for bacon, which in turn comes from the Latin *laridum*, bacon fat. The origin of the word suggests that the pig was the principal animal to be salted and stored for future use. An alternative to this expression was 'to make cold meat' of someone, but the allusion is the same.

Too many cooks spoil the broth

One of the most popular and often-quoted proverbs explains particularly well that if too many people are employed in one task the outcome is likely to be unsuccessful. A sixteenth-century version of the proverb runs: 'The more cooks the worse potage' – potage, or pottage, being a generic name for any sort of thick soup, whereas 'broth' generally has meat as an essential ingredient.

Upper crust

In days gone by loaves were baked directly on the floor of the oven, and consequently the lower part of the loaf became charred. This was cut off and fed to the menial domestic staff, while the top part, the 'upper crust' was offered to the most important guests. Figuratively it came to be a term for the aristocracy or higher echelons of society.

What's sauce for the goose is sauce for the gander

This has often been referred to as 'the woman's proverb', as it calls for equality between men and woman. It was first recognised in England in the seventeenth century, but is believed to have a much earlier provenance. As an aside, the traditional sauce for goose is made from apples, as the goose comes to maturity and is fit for killing at the same

The Laundry

Long before the invention of the modern washing machine, household washing was done in a stream. The clothes and household linen were soaked, pounded with rocks to loosen the dirt and then spread out on bushes to dry. In large households, by the Middle Ages, the washing was being done indoors in wooden tubs. The wet clothes would be stretched out on tables and wooden bats replaced rocks as a means of loosening the dirt.

By the sixteenth century the laundry, or lavendry, came into being as a stone-floored room complete with fires for heating water, tubs, tables and various accessories such as a dolly – a wooden appliance with projecting prongs used to stir the washing and press it against the side of the tub.

Laundry work was physically arduous and exhausting and remained so until well into the twentieth century. It was not until the invention of the electric washing machine, and later still the tumble drier, that the drudgery was taken out of keeping the household clean and fresh.

'Doing the washing' is now a relatively very simple chore, but the familiar expressions relating to the task tend to come from the days when it involved a lot of sweat and toil and took up a great deal of time.

Beetle away

When someone is very busy indeed they are sometimes referred as 'beetling away'. The expression comes from the wooden bat that washerwomen used to beat clothes to remove dirt and grime. It was called a 'beetle' or a 'battledore' and sometimes, but not always, was used in conjunction with a wooden washing block. In the right hands, the beetle was amazingly effective and in Ireland it was in common use up until the twentieth century.

Clothes horse

This useful contraption has nothing to do with the animal but takes its name from a different sort of beast altogether. A flick through *The Shorter Oxford English Dictionary* will tell you that a horse is also 'a frame or structure on which something is mounted or supported'. There were various colloquial names for the structure, such as in Yorkshire where it was known as a 'winters-'edge'. In summer the peasants would spread their washing on the hedges to dry, but in winter the clothes had to be dried indoors, and so the 'hedge' had to be brought inside, hence the name given to the clothes horse. The use of the term to describe someone who has a passion for fashion and who likes to display his or her finery, first appeared around 1850.

Every tub must stand on its own bottom

This rather delightful Elizabethan expression means that there are some things you have to do for yourself and that cannot be done by others. The reference is to the solid tubs that were used for a variety of domestic chores, particularly in the laundry.

Iron out the wrinkles

The allusion in this expression is obvious. Pressure and heat applied to a garment is assured to 'iron out the wrinkles' and so the term came to be used to mean smooth out the difficulties of a situation.

It will all come out in the wash

This expression is used to pacify someone who is anxious about the outcome of a particular situation. The idea is that, in the way that hot water and soap remove dirt and stains, everything will be ultimately clarified and resolved. Therefore, there is no need for concern, it does not matter.

It won't wash

For the origin of this expression, one must go back to the days when printed calico was in vogue. If you were wealthy you could afford fabric woven with integral patterns, but if not an alternative was printed calico. The problem was that printed calico could not withstand any form of laundering for fear the pattern would be washed off. To say something 'wouldn't wash', therefore, was to imply that it was of little permanent value. Nowadays, the expression implies more that something 'will not hold water' and is said of an excuse or explanation that is obviously far-fetched or unbelievable. As an aside, the inferiority of the material that gave rise to 'it won't wash' is reflected in the name given to cheap, public dances: they were called 'Calico Balls'.

Leave in the suds

In much the same way that stained clothes or linen were left to soak, someone who was 'left in the suds' was not rescued from a troublesome situation.

Sleep on a clothes line

While it sounds exceptionally uncomfortable, the person who professed to be able to sleep in such a position was claiming to be able to look after himself, unafraid of the hardship of roughing it. In reality, many poor mortals could lay claim to such mettle, as during the nineteenth century those who could not afford even the cheapest bed took what rest they could on the 'twopenny rope'. The down-and-outs would sit on a bench and lean forward against a line stretched tightly in front of them. In the morning the rope would be unceremoniously cut and the benches cleared.

Take the starch out of someone

No doubt there are a number of pompous and self-opinionated people we would enjoy seeing 'the starch taken out of', for in its polite form it merely means to deflate or 'take down a peg' (which in itself is a naval rather than a domestic expression). Starch was first introduced into England from France in the middle of the sixteenth century to support the fashion for extravagant ruffs. Quickly 'starch' became a synonym for 'stiff', as in manner, and we still refer to someone who is overly formal as being 'starchy'.

To be put through the mangle

This expression graphically explains having to endure a gruelling experience, to be 'wrung out'. The original contraptions, the earliest machinery to be used in the laundry, were boxes weighted with stones. These were moved backwards and forwards upon rollers to press sheets, tablecloths and other linen spread flat upon a table beneath. It was not until the nineteenth century that the hand-wringer became fashionable. Two rollers, initially of iron and later of wood, were held with weighted levers or screws to allow the clothes to be passed between them. Hand-operated mangles, in one form or another, were in common use well into the twentieth century when the spin dryer took over the chore.

To get lost in the wash

While we all know that certain items of clothing, socks in particular, have a propensity for getting lost in the wash, this expression stems not from the hazards of a domestic necessity but from a royal disaster. In 1216 a convoy of King John's horses and wagons were caught unawares and swallowed up by the incoming tide on the sands of the Wash. The expression still conveys the idea that something has just disappeared with neither rhyme nor reason.

To live by taking in one another's washing

If a group of people had no visible means of support, this was a term jocularly applied to explain their situation and how they managed to survive extreme poverty. Obviously 'taking in one another's washing' would be of no financial benefit and would provide nothing more than variety.

To wash one's dirty linen in public

The French have a saying that translates as 'wash your dirty linen at home', which could be seen as sound advice to someone who chooses to wash his or her dirty linen in public. But French or English, the phrase refers to the act of discussing discreditable elements of one's private life away from hearth and home, a habit considered to be ill-advised.

Too many irons in the fire

Now used to convey the idea that having too many projects on the go inhibits the success of any one of them, the expression comes from the days when irons needed to be heated in or on the fire. Smoothing out the wrinkles from freshly washed and dried clothes and linens was

first done by heating up smooth stones in the embers of a fire, and then wrapping them up in a cloth to protect the hands, before pressing them over the fabric. In time, stones were replaced by flat irons, which again were heated on a grid above a fire and later again upon a stove. To save time a busy laundress would heat up several irons simultaneously, but in doing so she risked them getting too hot and scorching or burning the clothes or linens being ironed.

Wash day

Monday was the traditional day to commence the lengthy chore of doing the laundry, if only to allow sufficient time during the week to get it dry, pressed, aired and ready again for use. To leave the task until later in the week was said to be indicative of bad housekeeping. A common rhyme about washing days ends with the couplet:

Wash on Friday, wash in need;
Wash on Saturday, a slut indeed.

To wash clothes on New Year's Day was to invite death to your door and washing blankets in May was equally dangerous. The worst day of all for doing any aspect of laundry work was Good Friday.

Washed out

Someone who is 'washed out' is totally exhausted. One only needs to think of the gruelling processes that laundry was subjected to in times gone by to appreciate how graphic this expression really is.

Wrap it up in clean linen

In the seventeenth century if you wanted to relay a particularly sordid story you might have chosen to 'wrap it up in clean linen'. It described the means of speaking delicately about an indelicate subject.

The Dining Room

Surprisingly, the formal dining room as a specialised room for eating in is a fairly recent household addition.

In medieval times people came together for meals in a communal 'hall', and many of today's expressions have their origins in the etiquette imposed by these large, ritualistic gatherings. The great economic and social changes of the seventeenth and early eighteenth centuries resulted in smaller households and thus a change in social eating patterns. The biggest and best room in the house, the dining room came about to serve as a showcase for the family's wealth and status. In time, it came to be seen as a masculine room due to the peculiarly English custom of the women leaving the men alone to drink, smoke and talk after the meal (regarded on the Continent as rather vulgar), which was often reflected in its décor as well as in related sayings.

Nowadays, formal dinners in a grand setting may seem consigned to history, but the tradition lives on in some of our everyday phrases.

A lot on one's plate

To overload one's plate in a literal sense is the height of bad manners and indicative of a glutton. Figuratively speaking, there is no such slur. The expression is used to describe the state of someone who is overburdened with work or worries.

Above and below the salt

At medieval feasts, where you sat in relation to the salt cellar was highly significant. The custom was to place a large cellar in the centre of the table for communal use. The most esteemed guests and members of the household would sit between the salt and the host, 'above the salt', and those of less importance sat 'below the salt'. In time, the expressions became verbal shorthand for indicating a person's perceived status in society.

Backhander

Now used to mean money given to obtain a favour, the expression 'backhander' is linked to the custom surrounding the drinking of port. Traditionally the port is passed to the left and from hand to hand. At a large dinner party a thirsty man might have to wait a while for his turn. Anyone who defied tradition and moved the port to the right to top up his glass was said to be guilty of a 'backhander'. The connotation was that the guilty party was concerned only with advantaging himself.

Bit of jam

There are various expressions linked to jam, most of which concern the sweetness of the product. In the nineteenth century, for example, a slang term for a very pretty girl was 'a bit of jam'; a wife was dubbed 'lawful jam'; and a sweetheart was referred to, among the lower classes, as a 'jam-tart'. 'Elderly jam' was a woman past her prime: 'Elderly jam is elderly jam, and Heaven preserve it, for man turns from it.' 'Real jam', on the other hand, was said to be 'cash and kisses'. The reference, of course, in all these sayings, is to the conserve of fruit and sugar which for hundreds of years was a luxury foodstuff. It was the cost of sugar, which was first introduced into Europe in the seventh century from Asia, that made jam so expensive. It was not until the seventeenth century, with the imports of the East India Company, that the price of sugar fell sufficiently to make it more readily available to the middle and lower classes.

Born with a silver spoon in one's mouth

The spoon alluded to is an Apostle Spoon, a traditional christening present from a godparent. The expression suggests, however, that a child born into a wealthy family would have no need to wait for such a gift for his first taste of luxury. A complete set of Apostle Spoons was, nonetheless, a generous gift. There are twelve, each with a different apostle at the top of the handle, and sometimes even an additional Master Spoon and Lady Spoon would be included.

Catch not a falling knife nor a falling friend

This rather uncharitable Victorian expression suggests that in either circumstance you risk being hurt. The inference is that to side with failure is somehow to bring disaster upon oneself.

Coffee

One of the most common of everyday drinks was introduced to England in 1636 but remained a beverage of the aristocracy well into the twentieth century. The word itself had gone through many permutations before reaching us in the seventeenth century and its roots are believed to be in some way connected to *Kaffa*, the region in the south Abyssinian highlands where the coffee tree is believed to have originated. The first coffee house in England opened in Oxford in 1650 and one of the recommended ways to prepare the exciting new drink was:

Roast the beans in an old frying pan until black right through.
Crush until fine and force through a muslin sieve.
Mix one ounce of the resultant powder with two pints of water and boil for fifteen minutes.

Companion

A common synonym for a friend or associate, the word takes its origin from the Latin *cum* meaning with and *panis*, bread. Therefore, someone with whom you share a meal can be said to be a true companion.

Cry roast meat

In the days when many people lived on meagre rations, roast meat was a treat worth shouting about, but to do so risked inviting thieves or unwanted guests. In the figurative sense, if a person 'cried roast meat' he was seen as a braggart. The added implication was that to boast of success is to risk losing it.

Cut the mustard

When someone is said to have 'cut the mustard' it means they have done a thing well, particularly when it was suspected beforehand that they might not. As well as being a popular condiment, mustard became a slang term for 'the best'. There is one school of thought that favours the idea that the 'cutting' relates to the harvesting of a notoriously difficult plant to glean, thereby implying that only the best can undertake the task. Another idea suggests that the term comes from the practice of adding vinegar to 'cut' or reduce the bitterness of the mustard seeds when creating the familiar paste. (The simile, 'as keen as mustard' alludes to the sharpness of the condiment.) Yet another notion is that the term is a confusion with the military expression 'cut the muster' which means well turned out both in appearance and punctuality. Whatever its origin, it is patently clear that *not* to 'cut the mustard' signifies a failure to achieve the required standard.

Dine with Duke Humphrey

Far from being entertained to a lavish meal, 'to dine with Duke Humphrey' meant going without dinner altogether. Humphrey, the Duke of Gloucester, was the youngest son of Henry IV and renowned for his generosity and hospitality. It was rumoured when he died that a monument would be erected to him in St Paul's. In reality it never was, but another tomb was popularly supposed to be his, and people seeking sanctuary within the church's precinct and consequently with no dinner to go to, would say that they were to 'dine with Duke Humphrey' that night. The expression was well understood in its day, as was a similar but later one, to 'sup with Sir Thomas Gresham'. Gresham was the merchant financier who founded and built the Royal Exchange, which, business apart, became a favourite haunt for loungers. Such habits were even later encapsulated in Robert Hayman's 1628 *Quodlibets*, which includes *Epigram on a Loafer*:

> *Though little coin thy purseless pocket line,*
> *Yet with great company thou are taken up;*
> *For often with Duke Humphrey thou dost dine,*
> *And often with Sir Thomas Gresham sup.*

Both expressions remained in common use until the early nineteenth century.

Dining room and dining room chairs

Rather than being a reference to a room and furniture, in colloquial use the 'dining room' was slang for 'mouth'; 'dining chairs' were consequently one's teeth.

Eat someone out of house and home

Although it was known centuries ago, this is still a common joking accusation of someone who has a more than healthy appetite and risks the family fortune by it. However, in Shakespeare's *The Second Part of Henry IV*, Mistress Quickly uses the expression more earnestly when accusing Falstaff: 'He hath eaten me out of house and home; he hath put all of my substance into that fat belly of his …'

Fruit salad

This is the rather irreverent slang term for the sets of beribboned medals worn by soldiers and ex-servicemen on special occasions.

Fork out

Still used as a common expression for 'pay up', 'fork out' has its roots in eighteenth-century thieves' slang. For them 'forks' were fingers, as indeed they were for the majority of the nation up until the seventeenth century. Although forks were used at royal and noble tables from the fourteenth century onwards for eating sweetmeats, most of the meal was eaten with the fingers (knives being used as an implement to spear meat from dishes). The general introduction of the fork into England is usually attributed to one Thomas Coryat who, having travelled extensively in Italy and seen their use there, published an account of the matter in 1611. Coryat's ideas were initially met with ridicule and forks were considered a superfluous luxury. For that reason forks were forbidden in convents long after they became established tableware elsewhere.

From the soup to the nuts

In reference to a full, formal dinner, 'from the soup to the nuts', means from beginning to end. Anything done is such a fashion would be done completely.

Give someone the cold shoulder

Used figuratively, this means to be reserved and unwelcoming. The common view is that it comes from the practice of the host who, rather than offering a sumptuous meal, serves cold shoulder of mutton for dinner (a meal usually reserved only for servants and the like) as a way of telling an unwanted guest that he has outstayed his welcome. Appealing as this explanation is, the more plausible is that it was a Scottish expression, of unknown origin, popularised by Walter Scott's use of it in his novel *The Antiquary*, in 1816: 'The Countess's dislike didna gang farther at first than just showing o' the cauld shouther', the 'cauld shouther' expressing the idea of a physical dismissive movement rather than a reference to cold meat. What is certain is that the expression was established in common parlance by the mid-nineteenth century.

Give pap with a hatchet

The soft, mushy food given to babies and invalids has been called 'pap' for centuries and a 'hatchet', as a name of a type of small axe, has an equally long pedigree. Put together in the phrase 'give pap with a hatchet' the defining characteristics of each are used in sharp contrast. The expression means to perform a kindness in an unkind way, or to punish someone under the pretence that you are being charitable.

Hand something to someone on a plate

This means to give someone an easy victory, and alludes to the fact that it is no trouble at all to reach for something offered on a platter by a servant.

Have a spoon in everyman's dish

When communal dining was an everyday occurrence, dishes were indeed shared. But to 'have a spoon in everyman's dish' meant to be involved in everyone else's business, and could well be used to describe a busybody.

He sups ill who eats all at dinner

This is a Victorian homily against being profligate with your means when you are young. The inference was that if you spent everything in your youth, you faced the prospect of destitution in old age. (A shorter but less elegant version of the expression is: 'Shod in the cradle, barefoot in the stubble'.)

He who sups with the devil should have a long spoon

Chaucer knew this expression and used it in *The Squire's Tale*, which he wrote in the fourteenth century. It advises caution when dealing with dangerous people.

In a Jam

When someone is in a predicament or a sticky situation, we say they are 'in a jam'.

The expression is not directly linked to the conserve of sugar and fruit, but comes directly from the verb 'to jam', meaning to squeeze or press. Indirectly, however, there may well be a connection, as no one is sure why 'jam' is called 'jam' and the supposition is that it stems from the same verb.

In a pickle

This is akin to being 'in a jam', although this term definitely has domestic origins and comes from the generic name for the liquid used to preserve vegetables and savoury fruits. Brine and vinegar are two of the most common pickles, and it is from them that the relish takes its name. To be 'in pickle', however, was a more serious matter for it meant to be suffering from venereal disease. Whether it derives from the first expression or the latter is unrecorded, but 'pickle manufacturer' was a slang term for a publisher of cheap, badly-produced books.

Leave some for the Duke of Rutland

For centuries children were encouraged to leave a little food on their plates, encouraged by the wisdom of the Bible, in which it states: 'Leave off first for manners' sake; and be not unsatiable, lest thou offend.' The family name of the Duke of Rutland was 'Manners', and thus his name became a substitute for the original noun.

Lick honey with your little finger

While this would never be countenanced in a literal sense, it advises that it is unwise to scoop up flattery and compliments unreservedly. It was also used to advise caution when dealing with unexpected good fortune.

Make a napkin of one's dish-clout

In the days when the class system was seen as the backbone of Britain, this was an expression used to describe the actions of a man who married one of his servants. A 'dish-clout' was a dishcloth and the inference was that a man who made such a misalliance was attempting to 'make a silk purse out of a sow's ear'.

Marmalade

There are a number of stories surrounding this most English of preserves, the most misquoted one suggesting a connection with Mary Queen of Scots. It is said that when the queen was feeling ill, her favourite 'pick-me-up' was a concoction of boiled oranges, quince and other fruits and that the order to the kitchen would be accompanied with the explanation that 'Marie' was 'malade'. Put the two together, it is said, and you have marmalade. Unfortunately the truth is far more prosaic. Now made mainly with Seville oranges and sugar, the jam was originally made from quinces and the Portuguese word for quince is 'marmelo'.

Meat and drink

Something that is a source of great enjoyment or pleasure can be described as being 'meat and drink', meat being used as a general term for food. It was a phrase known in Shakespeare's day, and indeed he used it in *As You Like It* when Touchstone says:

It is meat and drink to me to see a clown.

New wine in old bottles

Any experienced butler would tell you that to put 'new wine in old bottles' would be unwise, and in fact flies in the face of biblical wisdom. In Matthew 9:17 it says: 'Neither do men put new wine into old bottles: else the bottles break, and the wine runneth out, and the bottles perish.' Figuratively, the expression refers to the introduction of new ideas into an organisation that cannot assimilate them.

One man's meat is another man's poison

This ancient proverb has an echo in many languages around the world and emphasises that people and their tastes differ widely. It means that what is beneficial to one person could easily be harmful to another.

Over the mahogany

A rich and strong wood, mahogany was first brought to England from the West Indies as ships' ballast and it was not until the 1750s that it began to be imported in large quantities for making furniture – dining tables in particular. If a man said he was going to discuss something 'over the mahogany', it meant he was planning to discuss a subject with his wife over dinner. The expression, in northern homes, became 'with the mahogany', and so 'mahogany' became a slang word for wife. 'Under the mahogany', on the other hand, was not where a husband longed to be, but was slang for a friendly gathering or social occasion; and 'to decorate the mahogany' was to put money on the bar for a round of drinks in a pub.

Ploughman's lunch

Although it sounds as if it was a common term hundreds of years ago to describe a simple meal of bread, cheese and pickle, the description is very much of the twentieth century. It was a highly successful marketing campaign of the 1970s, initiated by the English Country Cheese Council.

Punch

Introduced from India, and popular since the eighteenth century, 'punch' takes its name from the fact that it was traditionally made from five ingredients: spirit, water, sugar, spice and lemon juice. The Hindi name for the drink is *panch*, meaning five. (The expression 'pleased as Punch' is not connected to the drink at all but comes from the antics of the hook-nosed puppet in the traditional Punch and Judy shows.)

Soup-and-fish

The slang term for a gentleman's evening dress comes about because, should he be so attired, the meal he was about to enjoy would normally include both courses. (More informal dining meant that one or other could be excluded.)

Spoilt as a lace tablecloth

The time and devotion it takes to create fine, hand-made lace has ensured it has always been a costly commodity. The allusion in this simile is to the care that was lavished on such a tablecloth, storing it carefully and using it only on special occasions. To be looked after equally well would be to be pampered indeed. Since the introduction of machine-made lace in the mid-nineteenth century this expression has rather lost its pertinence. Prior to that, lace-making was a major industry in Britain and in the later stages of the eighteenth century about a hundred thousand people were employed in it.

Spoons

The most common metaphor involving spoons, 'spoon-feed', is literally what you do for a baby, therefore it is easy to understand its figurative use when applied to giving so much help or assistance that the recipient has to make no effort at all. A 'spoon', however, was a silly flirt and 'to spoon' was to kiss and cuddle. The term may well have derived from the long-standing Welsh custom of 'loving spoons'. Usually made of wood and often whittled by only a penknife, a loving spoon was a token of affection and an offer of courtship. If a girl accepted such gift from a young man, the business could begin.

Storm in a teacup

When someone creates a fuss about a trivial or unimportant matter, he or she is said to have created a 'storm in a teacup', or as Shakespeare might have put it 'Much Ado About Nothing'. While seemingly founded in English domestic life, the expression can be traced back to a Latin expression, *excitare fluctus in simpulo*, which has been translated as 'raise a tempest in a ladle'. The Americans, on the other hand, talk about 'a tempest in a tea-pot'.

Taking the chair

Dining chairs, as we know them, did not become popular until the mid-sixteenth century. Prior to that, the most common form of seating was the bench and the settle. Most homes would have only one, or maybe two, individual chairs with arms and backs and these were for the use of the most important persons. Hence, the most distinguished visitor would be invited to 'take the chair' and could be described as the 'chairman'.

The cup that cheers

The reference is to tea and comes from a quotation by William Cowper, who in 1785 in *The Task* wrote:

> *And, while the bubbling and loud-hissing urn*
> *Throws up a steamy column, and the cups,*
> *That cheer but not inebriate, wait on each.*

The same knife cuts bread and fingers

Elizabethan wisdom would have you understand that a dangerous instrument cannot discriminate how it is used. The expression 'the same knife cuts bread and fingers' was a warning that to be involved in dangerous exploits carries the inherent risk of danger to oneself.

Take meat before grace

Now common practice, 'to take meat before grace' referred to enjoying conjugal pleasures before marriage and that was considered more than impolite.

Trencherman

The notion that the medieval lord ruled over an unruly table could not be further from the truth. The etiquette of dining followed a strict order and good manners were demanded from all. The food was served on 'trenchers', thick slices of stale bread, and someone who was noted to have a healthy appetite was known as a good 'trencherman'. A bad trencherman, on the other hand, was a glutton: someone who resorted to eating his trencher. As trenchers were usually distributed as alms, the act of eating one's trencher deprived the poor. The expression lasted until long after wood had replaced bread as the material for trenchers. The simile, 'as a trim as a trencher' is later in origin and refers to the clean and wholesome appearance of a newly turned wooden plate.

Trencher friends

The term is perhaps best described as a medieval and adult version of 'cupboard love'. 'Trencher friends' were people who cultivated friendships for the sake of sitting at a bountiful table and the other pleasures that might ensue.

The Drawing Room

The 'withdraught' or 'withdrawing' room first mentioned in the late fifteenth century was not the formal room we think of today. This relatively unimportant room attached to the main bedchamber of the householder evolved into a place where private meals could be taken or select guests received. With the changing status of the dining room in the eighteenth century, 'withdrawing' became 'drawing' and the room took on a formal function in its own right away from the bedchamber. Guests would assemble there before dinner and return after the meal for drinks and games, the women customarily arriving ahead of the men. Thus, in the same way as the dining room was perceived as a masculine space, the drawing room came to be seen as feminine. The Victorians further extended the drawing room's formality, using it to receive guests during the ritual of morning calls and for taking afternoon tea, the new meal of the day. Consequently, the drawing room has long been the home of polite, and no doubt often inane, conversation, and many of its associated phrases reflect this.

Afternoon tea

The Victorian love of taking 'afternoon tea' led to the common description of such sectors of society where it was favoured as 'afternoonified', meaning smart. For many a Scottish schoolboy, however, the prospect of 'afternoon tea' was not a pleasant one, as it was a euphemism for detention.

Antimacassar

The fashion for hair oil in Victorian times put many prized pieces of furniture at risk, so covers were devised to throw over the backs of chairs and sofas to protect them. The rather grand name for such a simple item comes from the fact that 'Macassar' was the brand name of a particularly popular hair oil, and the covers were designed to act against or 'anti' it.

Break the teapot

In the Victorian era, moderation in all things was admired, if not always maintained. If someone changed their habits and eschewed abstinence for alcohol, he was said to have 'broken the teapot'.

Bric-à-brac

In France a 'marchand de bric-à-brac' is someone who sells things such as old screws and odds and ends of little worth, but the Victorians classified 'bric-à-brac' as far more valuable. It was, and still is, the name given to an assortment of ornaments and curios. The term comes from an obsolete French term, *à bric et à brac*, meaning 'at random'. In modern French, *un bricoleur* is an odd-job man.

Chesterfield

Philip Dormer Stanhope, the fourth Earl of Chesterfield, may have given his name to a long overcoat with a velvet collar that became fashionable in the eighteenth century, but it is unlikely that he was personally responsible for a furniture vogue a hundred years later. A Chesterfield is a particular style of upholstered sofa that has arms and back at the same height. It is considered more likely that the furniture took its name from the Derbyshire town where it was first made.

Chintz

This rather extraordinary word began life as *chint*, the Hindi name for the painted calicoes imported from India in the seventeenth century. (The Hindi word comes from the Sanskrit for 'variegated'.) The popularity of the fabric for soft furnishings meant that other manufacturers copied it and soon there was a range of 'chints' on the market. Eventually, the plural was adopted as a singular noun and the final fanciful spelling ended up as we write it today. Modern chintz tends to be fast-printed glazed cotton of lavish floral design, but the adjective 'chintzy' is a slightly disparaging term meaning fussy or garish.

Curtains

Most of the expressions in English relating to 'curtains' are theatrical in origin, but when the word is used as a euphemism for death it has domestic connotations. It was customary, and still is in many parts of England, to draw the curtains of a house on the day of a neighbour's funeral as a mark of respect.

Doily

The small decorative napkin, which since the latter half of the twentieth century has also been made from paper, began life in a celebrated draper's shop in the Strand. The Doyleys made their fortune from supplying material that was 'at once cheap and genteel', according to the *Spectator* in 1712, and originally were known for a light fabric used for summer wear and 'doyley petticoats'. Doily (an alternative spelling of the name) napkins became very popular in the nineteenth century as mats to place under cakes on a plate or stand.

Earl Grey

The drawing room in the Victorian era became the setting for the increasingly elaborate ritual of 'afternoon tea' and a popular blend of tea was 'Earl Grey'. It is said to have taken its name from the second Earl, Charles Grey, who was to be Prime Minister from 1830–34 under William IV. It is reputed that a consignment of tea was forwarded to Grey by a Chinese dignitary as a thank you present for British intervention in a particular matter. The tea in question was a blend of Assam and Ceylon, scented with oil of bergamot (which belongs to the citrus family). Soon after, 'Earl Grey' was being produced commercially and enjoyed, as it still does, considerable success.

Fumed oak

Furniture made from 'fumed oak' – oak that has been exposed to ammonia vapours to darken it – became very popular in the early nineteenth century. Noel Coward used the term as a name for one of his plays, and in doing so contributed to 'fumed oak' becoming a synonym for 'suburban'. To describe something as 'fumed oak' was to suggest that it was typically middle-class and therefore not necessarily desirable.

Grandfather clock

Prior to the travels of an American songwriter called Henry Work in the 1870s, the imposing weight and pendulum eight-day clocks in tall cases, were known predominantly as 'floor clocks'. The change in name came about because Mr Work was told a story while staying at a hotel in North Yorkshire. The pub had been owned by two brothers who owned a floor clock that kept remarkably good time for many years. When one of the brothers died the clock started losing time and finally stopped once and for all (although fully wound) when the second brother died at the age of ninety. Henry Work was so inspired he wrote a song, based on the story, that includes the lines:

> *Oh, my grandfather's clock was too tall for the shelf,*
> *So it stood ninety years on the floor.*
> *It was taller by half than the old man himself,*
> *Though it weighed not a pennyweight more.*

More than a million copies of the sheet music were sold, and thereafter 'floor clocks' became generally known as 'grandfather clocks'. 'Grandmother clock' is the common name for the shorter, pinch-waisted version of a grandfather clock.

Mantelpiece

The glorious masterpieces of architects such as Robert Adam are a far cry from the original intention. The first mantelpieces were simply shelves above a fireplace with pegs from which to hang wet mantles and other garments. The spelling of 'mantel' is a variation of the more common 'mantle' but is closer to the Latin source word, *mantellum*, meaning cloak.

On the carpet

Just to be confusing this expression could be used in two ways. On the one hand it was used in the sense of calling someone to account for his misdeeds. On the other, it meant that something was under consideration or likely to happen – a version of 'on the cards' (which refers to Tarot or fortune-telling cards). The first carpets were brought to England from the East during the Crusades, but were used as table and bed covers rather than put on the floor. Originally a carpet was simply a form of rough cloth made of threads unravelled from a previously used piece of fabric. In the fifteenth century pieces of 'carpet' were laid on floors for people to kneel or sit on, and those who could afford to do so took to leaving them down permanently. Gradually the word became specific to floor-covering, especially as the use of rushes and straw for the purpose died out.

Parlour

Originally a parlour was a room set aside in a monastery where the monks could talk to lay visitors. The word comes directly from the French, *parler*, to speak. In fourteenth-century private homes the parlour was a room set aside for convivial conversation and, later, for receiving guests. As time progressed, the parlour became a male preserve, while the women took dominance in the withdrawing room. By the nineteenth century the name was applied to the 'best' room in the homes of the middle and lower classes. Such parlours tended to be used only on Sundays, high days and holidays or as a place to entertain important guests.

Parlour-boarder

Rather than being a guest who was lodged in the best room in the house, a parlour-boarder was a boarding-school pupil who had his meals with the teacher's family. Such privilege, of course, carried the burden of extra fees.

Parlour tricks

A slightly derisive term for social accomplishments. When young men were warned against using 'any of their parlour tricks here' the implication was that they should attempt to be a little more sincere.

Poker to draw up a fire

In the days when evil spirits and hobgoblins were the dread of common folk and lords alike, it was believed that to place the poker across the front of the grate with its point towards the chimney would make the fire draw. In reality the action had no effect whatsoever on the efficiency of the fire but created the shape of the Cross, against which all spirits are helpless. The primary concern was to keep the house spirit, Lob, at bay, as he was inclined to lie by the fire and instigate mischievous pranks.

Put a sock in it

This impolite way of asking someone to quieten down is said to come from the days of wind-up gramophones, where the sound came out through a horn. In lieu of a volume control, it was said that a sock was the most efficient way of muffling the sound.

Sofa

The English word sofa dates from about 1625 and comes via the French from the

Arabic, *suffa*, which was a raised part of the floor covered with carpets and cushions. By the early eighteenth century, the long stuffed seats designed for reclining or sitting upon were commonplace. The poet, William Cowper, was moved enough to write:

> *Thus first necessity invented stools,*
> *Convenience next suggested elbow-chairs,*
> *And luxury the accomplished sofa last.*

Sweep under the carpet

If there is something you would like put out of sight or hidden away, then you could always resort, figuratively speaking, to sweeping it under the carpet. Considered in its literal sense to be the habit of a lazy housewife or maid, who disdained from bending to collect the dust she had amassed with her broom, the figurative use gained popularity in the nineteenth century.

Teaboardy

Today we dismiss paintings we think inferior as 'chocolate-boxy', a term that recalls the days when confectionery was sold in packages resplendent with landscape or village scenes. The Victorians used a different point of reference but the meaning was the same. Tea-boards were old-fashioned tea trays decorated with painted landscapes and a picture described as 'teaboardy' was one not generally regarded to be high in artistic merit.

The tea and sugar

Essential as they are to any afternoon party, in this instance 'the tea and sugar' was the name given to a supply train. The one in question was that which fed and watered the builders of the Transcontinental Railway in Australia during the 1920s.

Wainscot

Originally the word wainscot meant planks or boards used for making wagons, and is thought to be a derivation of the Middle Low German 'wagenschot', which meant just that. Initially in England the word was used to describe quality oak imported from Russia, Germany and Holland for fine panel work. By the mid-sixteenth century 'wainscot' was used as a general term to describe any wood panelling used to line the walls of a room.

Whatnot

There is no definitive reason as to why a small piece of furniture should be given such a delightful name, but it could be that the stand, with shelves one above the other for displaying a variety of items, took its name from the term 'whatnot' which was in common parlance from the early sixteenth century. The expression was used to describe anything whatsoever, or an accumulation of all sorts of things – such as might be displayed on the open shelves of the stands that were so popular in Victorian households.

The Bedroom and Beyond

The privacy we enjoy, and expect, in our bedrooms would have astounded our ancestors. For centuries communal sleeping was the norm, and even the private chambers of the noble were far from private. Although 'bedchambers' became common in the mid-sixteenth century, they were still used for a great deal of business other than sleeping. It was during the eighteenth century that the bedchamber was pushed upstairs to make way for more reception rooms on the ground floor, much like the bedrooms of today.

Unfortunately, with early privies, close-stools, chamber pots and the original water closets all falling foul of England's inadequate drainage system, our response to the demands of nature has, historically, been less successful. The Victorians, with their principle of 'cleanliness is next to godliness', eventually created the first truly efficient bathrooms and lavatories. The inherently intimate activities of the bedroom and beyond have given us a wealth of expressions where euphemism reigns supreme.

Apple-pie bed

Making an 'apple-pie' bed has been a favourite practical joke of school-boys for years, but the name of the prank has little to do with apples or pies. The exact origin of the expression is unknown but it is thought to derive from the French, *nappe pliée*, meaning folded sheet or tablecloth.

Beauty sleep

While we now use the term 'beauty sleep' as a general expression for any time spent in bed, originally it was quite specific. Sleep taken *before* midnight was considered to be the most beneficial to one's looks. Young people who ventured to stay up later were warned of the adverse effect such wanton habits would have on their looks.

Bed turning

There are numerous superstitions surrounding the positioning of beds in general and the turning of mattresses in particular. The inauspicious days vary around the country but Sunday and Friday are usually regarded as unlucky. If the task is performed on the former it is likely to give you bad dreams for the coming week, and if you do so on the latter you risk a variety of evils, including turning a ship at sea. The way in which you turn a bed is also held to be significant, especially in Oxfordshire where a local rhyme suggests:

> *If one day you would be wed,*
> *Turn your bed from foot to head.*

Between you, me and the bedpost

This is an earlier version of the 'between you and me and these four walls' and is said usually when the speaker is about to divulge a piece of tittle-tattle or gossip. The inference is that as the bedpost is an inanimate object in a private room, there is little chance of the communication being repeated.

Bolster up

A bolster is a long pillow or cushion that stretches across the bed and is used to support individual pillows or cushions. Therefore, to 'bolster' someone or something up is to lend extra support or encouragement and the expression has been used in this figurative sense since the early sixteenth century.

Born on the wrong side of the sheet/blanket

This was just one of the more gentle ways of saying that a person was illegitimate. Another popular phrase was to say that such a child 'came through the side-door', or 'in at a window'.

Boudoir

This room where a woman could retire to be alone or entertain her most intimate friends takes its name from the French, *bouder*, to sulk. It was in the Palace of Versailles during the reign of Louis XV that such rooms were established for the king's mistresses. In eighteenth-century England the term was commonly applied to the sitting room of the lady of the house, whether or not she had a tendency to ill-humour.

Cat's pyjamas

The origin of this delightful expression is unknown but thought to have come to England from America. It is a variation of the 'cat's whiskers' or the 'bee's knees' and is used to say that something is excellent or worthy of praise. Real pyjamas, those not worn by cats, were brought back to England by travellers from India at the end of the eighteenth century. *Pajama* in Hindi is the name for the loose, baggy trousers worn as daywear by Muslims. The Hindi word comes from the Persian, *pa* meaning leg, and *jama* meaning garment. Either for climatic reasons or out of a sense of propriety, the English added a matching jacket but kept the original name. Eventually 'pyjamas' took over from nightshirts as the most popular sleeping attire for men; and in the latter half of the twentieth century women also adopted the fashion.

Curl paper condition

The long and luxurious ringlets loved by women through the ages have been achieved in a variety of ways but the most common was to twist the hair around strips of cloth.

Later strips of toilet paper were used and these were euphemistically called 'curl paper'. Curls newly released from being wrapped in paper are at their best and if left too long will drop and fall. Therefore, to say something is in 'curl paper condition' is to say it is immediately ready.

Curtain lecture

One has to envisage a fully draped four-poster to understand why this is the term used to describe a private reproof of a husband by his wife once they are alone and the curtains on the bed are drawn. Dryden was so disdainful of the habit he wrote:

> *Besides what endless brawls by wives are bred,*
> *The curtain lecture makes a mournful bed.*

In 1886 such scoldings also became known as Caudle Lectures, from a series published in *Punch* in which a character, Mr Caudle, suffered the nagging of his wife once they had retired to bed.

Down the drain

Something that is lost forever or been wasted is said to have gone 'down the drain'. Considering the inefficiency of the early English drainage system, it is a wonder that this expression ever caught on. Attempts at installing effective drainage systems into the grand houses of yesteryear were very much a case of 'hope over experience', and it was not until well into the nineteenth century that there was some genuine progress in the whole process.

Everyone stretches his legs

The full proverb runs, 'Everyone stretches his legs according to the length of his coverlet' and suggests that the majority of people will live to the full extent of their means. In 1300 the financial warning was that he 'who stretches further than his blanket will reach, in the straw his feet he must stretch'.

Eye-wash

The allusion in this expression is to something that blinds someone to what is really happening and anyone accused of talking 'eye-wash' has uttered nonsense or drivel. It is also used to refer to something that is done, not for any practical purpose, but purely for effect. Like so many expressions in the English language, the exact origin is unknown.

Feather bed and pillows

In the mid-nineteenth century, any woman deemed to be fat was described as a 'feather bed and pillows', the inference being she would afford a man a good night's sleep.

Go through with a fine-tooth comb

Anyone who has had to deal with a louse-infected head will appreciate how thorough and painstaking a search with a 'fine-tooth comb' really is. The expression refers, of course, to the use of a nit comb, which has exceptionally thin and closely set teeth.

Go to bed in one's boots

There are scores of expressions to describe getting very drunk – and this is just one that was current in the nineteenth century. If someone made 'indentures with his legs', he was only tipsy. Either might be a consequence of having gone 'on the fuddle', a common term for a drinking bout. 'To die in one's boots' was a different matter altogether as it meant to be hanged or killed in a violent manner.

God looks to clean hands, not to full ones

The Victorian principle of 'cleanliness is next to godliness' is, perhaps, one of the factors behind this saying. It warns those to whom it is said of the dangers of being greedy and of seeking wealth above purity.

Hand washing

There are various expressions that stem from the washing of hands, some well known and some less so. 'To have clean hands', for example, implies that you have never taken a bribe and are above reproach. 'One hand will not wash the other for nothing', suggests, however, that a service will not be forthcoming unless payment is made. 'To make one hand wash the other' is relevant in the commercial world and refers to the practice of using one section of a business to support another to make it more competitive. 'One hand washes the other' is similar to 'you scratch my back, I'll scratch yours' and suggests that friends should help each other and so much the better if, in doing so, there is mutual benefit.

He will not put off his doublet before he goes to bed

This rather fanciful expression means that a man would not part with his property before he died – a much-applauded precaution. It was echoed in a saying that was part of the common wisdom in Gloucestershire: 'Take not off your clothes before going to bed.'

Hit the sack

For many people the luxury of a proper bed was beyond their means. In such instances makeshift mattresses would be made by stuffing sacks with straw. 'To hit the sack', therefore, is merely to go to bed. The expression has lasted long after such rudimentary beds were commonplace.

Hours of sleep

The customary answer today as to how much sleep one needs is usually 'ten minutes more', but in times gone by it was far more precise. An old proverb, often quoted by George III, said that what was required was: 'Six hours' sleep for a man, seven for a woman and eight for a fool'. The *Spectator* in 1908 was moved to suggest that on such a basis 'thousands of great men were, and are, fools'.

In the straw

Before the introduction of feather bedding, the usual stuffing for a mattress was straw and a woman said to be 'in the straw' was in childbirth. To be 'called to straw' was to be pregnant. It is thought that the expression referred to the practice of women stripping the bed to give birth in consideration of the problems involved in removing stains from blankets and linen. Even once feather beds were customary, in Norfolk it was considered extremely unlucky to give birth on a feather mattress in case it contained doves' or pigeons' feathers. If that were to be the case and the woman died, it was believed that such feathers would increase her suffering.

In the twinkling of a bedpost

To do something in 'the twinkling of a bedpost' means to do it immediately or as soon as possible. 'Twinkling' in this sense means a rapid twist or turn and the expression comes from the days when bedsteads often had removable staves incorporated into the bedstead to keep the bedclothes from falling off. These staves could easily be removed, and often were, so as to be used to beat and clean the bedding and mattress or to be used as a weapon.

Laugh like a drain

One only needs to consider how noisy the plumbing is in many old houses to appreciate how apt this expression is. To 'laugh like a drain' is to laugh very loudly and coarsely, in such a way as to remind the listener of water gurgling down a plughole.

Lay up in lavender

In the sixteenth century, the flowers and stalks of the popular plant, *Lavandula vera*, were held to have preservative qualities and were laid among linen and clothes put away in store to protect them from moths. To 'lay up in lavender' therefore, was to put something away carefully for future use. In slang terms it meant 'to pawn' and a pawnbroker was known on the streets as a 'lavender-cove'. In the nineteenth century it took on the additional meaning of putting away in the sense of 'imprisoning', the premise being that a person 'laid up in lavender' was out of the way of doing harm. In his 1822 novel,

The Fortunes of Nigel, Sir Walter Scott used the expression in just this sense: 'Lowestoffe is laid up in lavender only for having shown you the way into Alsatia.'

Let every man soap his own beard

Over the centuries there have been many expressions centred on the call for everyone to look after his own affairs, and this is yet another. It implies that we must all be accountable for what we do and should not rely on others.

Loo

Why loo has become a popular term for lavatory has amused and puzzled etymologists for years. It is generally accepted that the word did not come into common use until the 1920s but many of its proposed origins are much earlier.

The most quoted is that it comes from the French, *gardez l'eau*, or 'mind the water', which was the popular cry when chamber pots were emptied out of the window onto the street below. Another idea is that is a contraction of 'Waterloo', used as a waggish alternative to 'water closet' – but again, that great battle preceded common usage of the word by more than a hundred years. The current supposition is that 'loo' comes from the French, *lieux d'aisances*, which translates as 'places of ease', a euphemism for lavatory. It has been suggested that the term would have become familiar to British serviceman fighting in France during the First World War.

Necessary woman

No doubt there are many misogynists who would consider this a contradiction in terms, but they may also be tickled to learn that a 'necessary woman' was a servant responsible for emptying and cleaning the privy. The name came about because in the seventeenth and eighteenth centuries the water closet or privy was known as the 'necessary house'. Through some unaccountable twist, in the twentieth century the term 'necessary' became a slang term for money, synonymous with another colloquial expression, 'the wherewithal'.

Netty

There have been various words in English for the lavatory, and 'netty' is just another. It was used in the north of England and is from the Italian, *gabinetti*, which is used, among other things, to describe water closets.

Never choose your women or linen by candlelight

The sound advice contained in this proverb was appreciated in the mid-sixteenth century. It suggests that the decisions concerning the two most important elements of a man's life should be made in broad daylight, rather than in the flattering glow of a candle flame.

Nightmare

It was not until the mid-sixteenth century that the word 'nightmare' took on its current meaning. Before that it was the name of an evil female spirit who sat on sleepers' chests and created a sense of oppression. In Old English, *mære* was a word for 'incubus'. The connotation of a 'nightmare' as being a frightening object or situation is a much later extension of the word.

Out of the top drawer

Maybe because it was often, literally, the place in a chest of drawers where you kept your most favoured possessions, in its figurative sense the term came to represent 'the best', as well the 'upper class'. In time the expression widened to include 'the hankie drawer' – again referring to the top drawer of a chest where such small items were stored, but this time being used in particular reference to the higher echelons of society. In a disparaging way someone would be referred to as 'not being out of the hankie drawer', that is to say he was not a born member of the upper classes.

Pillow securities

This term was used to describe safe investments. The notion was that any investor who had his money so tied up could afford to sleep easy in his bed.

Powder one's nose

This euphemism for a visit to the lavatory is, for obvious reasons, an expression mainly used by women. It came into common use in the early decades of the twentieth century. Prior to that, no self-respecting woman would publicly admit to using make-up, albeit that the majority did.

Quilts

The comfort of snuggling *under* a soft quilt was denied to those who were fortunate enough to own such an article centuries ago. Originally, quilts, from the Latin word for mattress, *culcita*, were used for lying on and were used on top of harder mattresses. By the nineteenth century the quilt had firmly changed places and was known as a bed cover, or counterpane (from the word *pane* meaning panel), the stuffing of which was held in place by cross-stitching.

Scabby heads love not the comb

The treatment for various diseases is one of the least appealing aspects of life in the sixteenth and seventeenth centuries and this expression relates to one of the milder ones. Should you suffer from any scalp irritation the answer was to comb your hair vigorously, irrespective of the irritation it may cause. ('Scabby' was also slang for vile or contemptible.) Used metaphorically 'scabby heads love not the comb' is to say that the people most in need of correction or constructive criticism are usually the least tolerant of such.

Sew pillows under people's elbows

While to 'sew pillows under people's elbows' sounds like a Heath Robinson idea of comfort, the expression actually dates from the fourteenth-century Wycliffe Bible. It means to give someone a false sense of security. The expression gained favour again in the seventeenth century, thanks to the use of it by the Restoration playwright William Wycherley, who was famed for his bawdy works.

Shampoo

The origin of the word 'shampoo' is from the Hindi, *campna*, meaning 'to press' and until the mid-nineteenth century, a 'shampoo' was a complete body massage which sometimes, but not always, culminated in having one's hair washed. However, once the word became associated with liquid hair-washing products, the noun soon became specific and the verb followed suit almost immediately.

Sleep like a top

It is often said that when you sleep deeply and soundly you 'sleep like a top'. Commonly, the allusion is put down to the seeming momentary pause of a spinning top when it rotation is at its height. However, there is another, rather more plausible explanation. The Italians have a saying that expresses the idea of a deep and peaceful slumber: *Ei dorme come un topo*. Translated it means 'he sleeps like a mouse'. *Topo* is the generic name and the Italian expression relates to the dormouse, that most somnolent of mice.

Sleep on a bag of saffron

The most treasured of medieval herbs, saffron was believed to be especially exhilarating, and if you were said to have 'slept on a bag of saffron' you were thought to be a particularly happy and merry person. (You would also need to very well off, as saffron was extremely expensive.) The herb comes from the stigma of the saffron crocus and about seventy-five thousand flowers were needed to produce a mere pound of the delight. A native of Asia, the crocus was acclimatised in Spain during the tenth century and was known in England three hundred years later.

Sleep tight

'Sleep tight, don't let the bedbugs bite' has been a catchphrase for years but the origin of the saying has never been pinpointed. There are those who favour the idea that it stems from the days when bed frames were strung with taut ropes to support the mattress. A sloppy rope would lead to discomfort and therefore a 'tight' rope was called for to ensure a good night's sleep. The dissenters will argue that, while such an explanation sounds plausible, the expression 'sleep tight' was not known until the nineteenth century when rope beds had passed out of fashion.

Soft soap

That 'soft soap' can be used as a term for flattery, is a reflection of the luxurious froth and bubbles such soap creates. The more common soap was made of a mixture of vegetable or animal fats and 'lye', a

strong alkaline solution often made from the ashes of the household
fire. Such soap was reasonably efficient but harsh on the skin and those
who could afford it bought soaps imported from Venice and Spain,
particularly the fine white soap of Castile.

The best mirror is an old friend

The thinking behind this expression is that if you really want to see
yourself you should rely on someone who not only knows you well but
also will be honest enough to tell you the truth. The reflective quality
of a mirror is an obvious metaphor for anything to do with self-
analysis or the analysis of others and, as such, has been used for
thousands of years. The earliest mirrors were made of polished metal
and examples have been found in England dating back to the Iron
Age. The glass mirrors we are more familiar with were introduced in
the Middle Ages from Constantinople, although they were the work of
Venetian craftsmen. The first mirrors to be made in England were
also made by Venetian glass-makers, who established workshops in
Lambeth, under the patronage of the Duke of Buckingham.

Throw the baby out with the bath water

This saying is a direct translation of a German proverb, and suggests
that the valuable and essential item can be lost through indiscriminate
or rash change. It was known in England in the early years of the
seventeenth century, even though taking a bath then was not an
everyday experience. Queen Elizabeth, for example, was said to take a
bath once a month 'whether she need it or not', but for many of her

subjects taking a bath was an annual event at best. In the poorer households the bath water would be shared, with the various members of the family taking their turn. As large families were not uncommon the water must indeed have been murky by the time the baby was immersed, and one can understand more clearly the basis for the expression.

Warming-pan

The long-handled metal pan full of hot charcoal was in common use in England for airing and warming beds in the fifteenth century, but the first slang use of it came a couple of hundred years later. At the time of the Restoration of King Charles II, a 'warming-pan' was a derogatory term for a female bedfellow. During the reign of his brother, James II, his followers, the Jacobites, were called 'The Warming Pans', the nickname stemming from the story that the King's son was introduced into the Queen's bed in a warming-pan, her own child having been stillborn. Even later, the term was coined by public schoolboys who would often send their juniors or 'fags' to warm up their beds on cold nights. At the same time, it was used to refer to someone who held open a position until someone more qualified or better suited to the post took it up.

Wash one's hands

The term is yet another euphemism for going to the lavatory. However, it closely reflects that originally lavatories were indeed simply rooms that had washing facilities. The word comes directly from the Latin, *lavare*, to wash.

Wash one's hands of something or someone

The allusion in this expression has nothing to do with domestic arrangements, but comes instead from Pilate's act of washing his hands during the trial of Jesus. In Matthew Chapter 22:24 it says: 'When Pilate saw that he could prevail nothing, but that rather a tumult was made, he took water, and washed his hands before the multitude, saying, I am innocent of the blood of this just person: see ye to it.'

The phrase, therefore, succinctly says that the person concerned will have nothing more to do with a matter with which he had previously been concerned.

Well-lathered is half-shaven

It has long been recognised that 'failure to prepare is preparation for failure' and this expression echoes those sentiments. It says that a job well prepared is already half-finished and comes from the days when a good barber prided himself on his ability to lather his client sufficiently well to make the shaving a rapid and easy process.

Wet blanket

For centuries, a person whose lack of enthusiasm spoils other people's pleasure or causes social discomfort has been labelled 'a wet blanket' and the expression alludes to the use of a wet blanket to dampen down a fire. The origins of the term 'blanket', however, are more interesting. Originally the name 'blanket' referred to an undyed woollen fabric that was used in a variety of ways. We know the French word *blanc* to mean white, but the English derivation 'blank' could mean just what it says, or white or grey. Perhaps because the fabric was so suitable for the task, the term blanket came to be used exclusively from the early fourteenth century for the warm bedcovers we know them to be. However, it is also claimed that the covers are so named because a Mr Thomas Blanket of Bristol was the first manufacturer of the items. If that is the case, one can but delight in the wonderful coincidence of his surname.

Wrong side of the bed

When someone gets up in a bad mood, he or she is said to have 'got out of the wrong side of the bed'. On a more literal level, the 'wrong' side was considered to be the left, and to get out on the left side of the bed was to invite misfortune. You only need to remember that our word 'sinister' is the Latin word for 'left', to appreciate the suspicion there was of a left-handed person or the left side of anything. For that reason it also was considered unlucky to put the left foot to the floor first or to put on the left shoe first.

The
Dressing Room

Although said to have first appeared in the seventeenth century, the 'dressing room' would have existed in some form before then. Despite a brief fashion for women to dress in the bedchamber, as on the Continent, in England husband and wife had separate dressing rooms. Given the elaborate clothing of the time, this was the most sensible arrangement. In grand houses, the guest rooms also had dressing rooms where ladies could spend time either alone or with their hostess before the day's events. For men, the dressing room took on the role of private study. During the late eighteenth century, many of the social and business activities that had previously taken place in the dressing room were relocated to other rooms, and by the Victorian era it was simply the place where the man of the house dressed, or, if needs be, slept.

Nowadays, dressing rooms are considered an enviable, but mostly unnecessary, luxury. However, many everyday expressions recall those intricate and layered fashions of the past, when dressing required preparation, patience and, more often than not, assistance.

A bit of muslin

Rather than being a piece of a favoured cloth, 'a bit of muslin', was nineteenth-century slang for a woman or a girl. Muslin itself was the general name for any delicate woven cotton fabric much favoured for women's dresses. The word comes, via the French and the Italian, from the town of Mosul in Mesopotamia, where the material was first made and exported from in the Middle Ages.

Be bowler hatted

To 'be bowler hatted' was not a description of one's state of dress, but said that you had been prematurely discharged from the army, complete with a gratuity in lieu of the remaining years of your commission. The payment itself was referred to as a 'golden bowler', (an early version of a 'golden handshake') and was so called because, in army terms, the bowler was a symbol of 'Civvy Street', being the customary headgear of businessmen in the City. The famous London hatters, James Lock and Company, are said to have made the first 'bowler' hat in the 1850s. It was for a gentleman who thought a low curled-brim hat with a rounded crown would be more suitable for hunting than a top hat, which was conventionally worn. The name is said to be an Anglicised version of Beaulieu, the name of the felt makers who provided the material for the original hat. The name of the huntsman was William Coke, and in the millinery trade a bowler is still known as 'a Coke'. By the late 1860s, the bowler had moved into town and by the end of the First World War it was an essential part of every businessman's wardrobe.

Bee in one's bonnet

An earlier version of this expression was to have 'bees in the head' which does not have quite the same ring to it but conveys, all the same, that the sufferer is buzzing with an idea or obsession. To have a 'bee in one's bonnet' is not considered a fortunate state of affairs, but the real insect, conversely, has always been held in high regard. Considered to be the wisest of all insects – even in early Christian tradition, bees were thought to be the winged servants of God – there are many superstitions surrounding bees. It used to be thought, for example, that if a maiden could walk unscathed through a swarm of bees, it was a sure sign that she was a virgin.

Belt and braces

This can be said of any policy that offers a back-up as security should the main plan fail. Certainly it is hard to imagine that a pair of trousers kept in place by both methods would dare have the audacity to collapse around the wearer's ankles. The origin of the expression is unknown, but it is often claimed to be a favourite expression among engineers.

Best bib and tucker

This expression is still recognised as referring to one's best clothes. The bib in question is not that used to keep babies clean during mealtimes, but refers to the top section of an apron which has the same name. A tucker was a frill of lace or muslin which women wore over their dresses in the seventeenth and eighteenth centuries to cover their necks and shoulders. To be in one's 'best bib and tucker', came to mean to be in one's finery, irrespective of the actual garments involved.

Better to wear out shoes than sheets

This is a Victorian admonition against laziness and echoes the sentiments of an older, sixteenth-century, saying: 'Better it is to shine with laboure, than to rouste for idlenes.'

Bigwig

For a short period during the reign of Elizabeth I, wigs were fashionable for men, but it was not until the 1660s that the trend really took hold. In the early eighteenth century they gained their largest proportions and the larger the wig, the higher the man's status. The term 'bigwig' soon became a common tag for someone considered to be important.

Blazer

There are those who will have you believe that the name of the jacket commonly found in many men's wardrobes stems from the fact that the original 'blazers' were in bright, 'blazing' colours used to distinguish sports teams. Others will tell you that it is thanks to a certain J. W. Washington who was captain of the HMS *Blazer*. It is said he decided in 1845 to dress his crew in blue and white striped jackets, and that the style was rapidly taken up by rowing clubs and the like. The more conventional 'blazer'

these days is navy blue, which might add credence to the second theory.

Boiled shirt

The stiff-fronted shirt worn by men in the evenings was commonly known as a 'boiled shirt' because of the starching process. It was also the name given to someone who was smug, dull-minded or priggish.

Button law

There was an Act of Parliament, upheld during the reigns of William III, Queen Anne and George I, that made it illegal for a tailor to make, or indeed a man to wear, a suit that had anything other than brass buttons. The law was designed to support the Birmingham brass industry and should any tailor see fit to contravene it, he risked being fined forty shillings for every dozen buttons made of any other material. Whether connected or not it is difficult to say, but there was an expression 'to have his buttons on' which was applied to anyone considered particularly shrewd and alert.

Buttonhole

As a noun 'buttonhole' is not only a slot in a garment but also a flower or small nosegay worn on a jacket. But as a verb the connotation is quite different. If you 'buttonhole' someone you pin them down in conversation, usually boring them sideways in the process. The French, by the way, have exactly the same expression, *serrer le bouton*.

Cloak one's intentions

Even though cloaks were a common garment in England from the Anglo-Saxon period onwards, this expression, meaning to hide or disguise one's true intent, did not come into everyday speech until the early sixteenth century. Worn as outer garments by both men and women, the shape and length of cloaks has varied through the ages. In the mid-twelfth century, for example, Henry II introduced the French fashion for short cloaks and for doing so, earned the nickname 'Curtmantel'.

Dressed up to the nines

There are two explanations for why someone who is over-dressed for an occasion or dressed in a fussy manner should be said to be 'dressed up to the nines'. The first is based on 'nines' being a corruption of the Old English word for eyes, *eyne*. Someone dressed up to his or her eyes would be over-dressed indeed. The other theory is that as ten is the number associated with perfection, nine is just one step short and therefore excellent.

Eat one's hat

Any person who promises to undertake such a feat does so in the conviction that he will not be called on to see it through. It is often used to express the user's belief in the certainty of a future outcome. But while a 'hat' is obviously indigestible, a 'hatte' is not. An early form of meatball, hattes were made from a mixture of veal, dates, saffron and other spices, bound with eggs. It has been suggested that the 'hat' in the expression 'to eat one's hat', comes therefore, from the food and not the article of clothing.

Feather in one's cap

To earn a 'feather in one's cap' is to have done something that earns you praise or acclaim. Far from being rooted in sartorial fashion, the expression is believed to come from the custom of the ancient Lycians, later Asian cultures and North American tribes, who added a feather to their headwear for each enemy they killed.

Feel the collar

During the nineteenth century, the great age of euphemisms, someone who was 'feeling the collar' was someone who was sweating from the exertion of having walked too far or too fast. 'To get hot under the collar', on the other hand meant, and still does, to get angry or enraged, but to 'get one's collar felt' was to be arrested.

Felt

There is an intriguing story told about the development of 'felt', which for centuries has been widely used to make rugs, clothing and hats. It is claimed that Clement IV, prior to being made Pope in 1265, had been fleeing from persecutors when his feet became badly blistered. To ease the pain he put a layer of sheep's wool between the soles of his feet and his sandals. After several days the constant motion and the sweat from his feet caused the wool to become completely matted into a single piece of fabric. Once finally established in Rome, it is said that Clement used the discovery to establish a felt-making factory in the city. The English word for the material, however, is derived from the West Germanic, *feltaz*, meaning 'beaten'.

Furbelow

In the eighteenth century the frill or flounce attached to a woman's skirt or petticoat was known as a furbelow, from the Spanish word for the same thing, *falbala*. In time anything considered flashy or ostentatious was dismissed as being a 'furbelow'.

Fustian

A kind of coarse twilled cotton and linen mix, fustian was called 'mock velvet' because of its nap and gained its name from *Fostat*, the Cairo suburb from where it was originally exported. The fabric was particularly suited to the making of men's jackets but figuratively speaking became slang for someone who was bombastic or who used unnecessarily lofty and overblown language.

Get one's shirt out

While the garment belongs in the Dressing Room, the action does not. The expression means to become angry or quarrelsome. It is thought that it alludes to the idea of a man pulling his shirt from his trousers in readiness to strip for a fight. We still use a variation of the phrase in modern speech, when we refer to someone as being 'shirty' or bad-tempered.

Gingham

The origin of the name of a fabric we now tend to associate with tablecloths is debated. There is one school that adheres to the notion that the name for this checked or striped cotton material comes from *Guingamp* in Brittany where it was manufactured. The other proposal is that the word is Malay in origin, coming from *gingang*, meaning striped. Whatever the truth, 'gingham' was so commonly used to make umbrellas during the nineteenth century that the word became a colloquial term for just such an item. The fabric was also popular for making servants' and orphans' clothing.

Hair powder

The extraordinary fashion of whitening one's wig or hair stemmed from a group of balladeers at the famed Bartholomew Fair, who powdered their hair to look all the more ridiculous. The fashion, however, caught on, and hair powder became an important commodity – so much so that in November 1746, a hundred barbers were committed before the Commissioners of Assizes and fined twenty pounds each for having in their custody hair powder not made of starch, contrary to an Act of Parliament.

Hand in glove

When two people are said to be 'hand in glove' it refers to them being in collusion, usually with mischief in mind. The term refers to the snug fit of a glove, which we again use when we say something fits 'like a glove'. It was the Persians who first wore gloves and initially they were considered effeminate by other nations. Gloves were not common in England until the tenth century, and then only as accessories for the clergy and nobility. It took a further three hundred years for women to adopt the fashion.

Handle with kid gloves

The leather from the hide of young goats was considered the finest, and was one of the most expensive leathers to be used in the glove industry. Their delicacy and value meant that kid-leather gloves were kept to be worn when there was no danger of having to undertake any manual task. Therefore, anything or anyone that is given the 'kid-glove' treatment is handled with extreme tact and gentleness.

Headband

Now a common accessory, a headband would never be found in the dressing rooms of a great house, for originally a 'headband' was a strip of linen worn as a punishment in girls' schools. A number of such bands, complete with the relevant offence embroidered upon them, were found at a school in Hertford: they include such misdemeanours as 'Gossipping', 'Ill Temper' and 'Obstinate'.

His hat covers his family

Yet another undated expression, it means that a person is all alone in the world, without a relative to his name.

If the cap fits, wear it

This expression is still very common today and means that if a remark or description is applicable, then you should apply it to yourself. However, in a more literal sense, it might have been wise to check first, as there was a law that decreed just what headwear could be worn by people of different ranks. In the 1568 Bailiff's Accounts for Leominster, in Herefordshire, for example, there is an entry recording that several persons were fined for wearing caps beyond their station in life.

In one's shirt

Long before pyjamas were introduced into England, the most common form of night attire was simply a shirt. Eventually specific shirts were manufactured for the job and 'night shirts' came into being. However, well into the nineteenth century it was commonly understood that to be 'in one's shirt' was to be in one's nightwear.

In the catching of a garter

This is an earlier version of 'at the drop of a hat', and became popular in the seventeenth century as a way of saying 'instantly' or 'immediately'. Garters are thought to be of Celtic origin and were originally bands tied around the knee to keep stockings in place. Over the successive centuries, there were various slang expressions centred on garters, but few are repeatable. One that is, is Scottish in origin: 'to cast one's garter' is to catch a husband.

Knickers

Women's underpants have been called 'knickers' since the 1880s and got their name because of their similarity to the original 'knickers', which were men's knee-length trousers, more fully titled 'knickerbockers' since the 1850s. These baggy trousers resembled the knee-breeches worn by the Dutch settlers in America who were characterised and illustrated in Washington Irving's book, *History of New York*, 'written' by the fictional author, Deidrich Knickerbocker. While the word is still in use today as a term for women's underpants, the resemblance of today's garments to the original 'knickers' has long since disappeared.

Laugh up one's sleeve

There was a time when sleeves were so long and loose that it was quite possible to cover one's face if one wanted to hide one's expression. Figuratively, however, the expression means to laugh to oneself, especially in a derisory or dismissive manner.

Mobcap

The curious name of this white, round, indoor cap comes from a folklore character. It was the favoured headgear of Queen Mab of the Fairies who, having once been a dainty apparition, fell from grace in the sixteenth century and was reduced to the role of a slattern. It is from her dishevelled state that the name for the cap arose, as it was used in the eighteenth and early nineteenth centuries by women to cover hair that was not yet 'dressed'.

Mothballs

The damage caused by voracious moth larvae has long been known to man and there are even biblical references to clothes being 'moth-eaten'. Over the centuries various herbs and potions have been used with differing levels of effectiveness. The most expensive way to keep the pesky mites at bay was to store one's clothes and valuable hangings in cedar wood or camphor wood chests. The camphor laurel, *Cinnamomum camphora*, is a native of China and the wood had been used for thousands of years in the East to make storage chests. Not only was the wood appreciated for its beautiful grain but the strong and pungent fragrance worked wonders as an insect repellent. Such imported luxuries, however, were denied to all but the richest of families and lesser mortals were forced to rely on herbs such as lavender, which was held to have excellent preservative qualities, or things such as bog myrtle, hops and pepper. It must have been assumed that moths had particularly sensitive noses, as the majority of deterrents were chosen for their strong smell. One extraordinary Victorian recipe runs: 'One drachm of oil of cloves, and one half of a drachm of oil of carraway, to which add a gill of the best gin or whiskey, and also a piece of camphor the size of a filbert, let the whole remain twenty-four hours. With this sprinkle the goods, fold them ironed and put away.'

The more conventional mothballs, as we know them, came into being in the twentieth century and the primary ingredient was again camphor – again in its white, crystalline form. The common use of the natural pesticide lasted until cheaper and more effective synthetic pesticides replaced it. In England there are two species of moth that attack and damage textiles – the case-bearing clothes moth, *Tinea pellionella*, and the common or webbing clothes moth, *Tineola bisselliella* – and in both instances it is the larvae that cause the damage. This appears to have been common knowledge up until the eighteenth century as the word 'moth' was used only to describe these species and was used mainly in reference to the larva rather than the adult insect. (The term 'clothes worm' was a synonym for 'moth'.) It was Dr Samuel Johnson who seemed to have muddied the entomological waters, when in his dictionary of 1755 he defined a moth as: 'a small winged insect that eats cloths and hangings', thereby giving credence to the false notion that it is the moths that do damage rather than their larvae. In the twentieth century the noun became a verb. 'To mothball' now means to set aside or put away for future use.

Nightcap

Considering how much heat is lost through the head, it is not surprising that our ancestors favoured the wearing of a nightcap to keep out the cold. Just as a nightcap, in its literal sense, was considered essential for a good night's sleep, so indeed was the last drink, usually alcoholic, that preceded the whole process and thus shared its name.

Old cardi

Contrary to misconception, the term 'an old cardi' has absolutely nothing to do with what is considered by many to be the quintessential British garment. It was a Welsh term to describe natives of Cardiganshire, who were considered by their compatriots to be excessively thrifty to the point of stinginess. To call someone 'an old cardi' was, in Wales, to accuse them of being miserly. The garment sort of 'cardi', or more commonly 'cardie', takes its name from James Thomas Brudenell, who was the seventh Earl of Cardigan. This sartorial giant was reputed to be so keen for his regiment to be the smartest in the British Army that he paid ten thousand pounds a year from his own pocket to ensure dress standards were maintained. He also came up with the idea of a knitted woollen waistcoat to protect himself and his men from the bitter cold experienced during the Crimean War. And so it was that the cardigan came into being.

Plus fours

The freedom afforded by knickerbockers became much appreciated as wear for outdoor sports in the early part of the twentieth century, and in the 1920s they were considered particularly suitable for golf. The name 'plus fours' comes from the extra four inches of cloth that tailors needed to ensure there was adequate fabric to overhang the leg-band. For a similar reason, the breeks favoured by the shooting fraternity are known as 'plus twos', being narrower in the leg and thus requiring not so much additional fabric.

Pocket an insult

This is another way of saying 'turn the other cheek'. The person who 'pockets an insult' receives and disregards a slur at the same time. Such a person could also be said to have 'put his pride in his pocket', as the term is applicable to anyone who puts personal vanities aside in a given situation.

Poplin

A popular fabric for centuries, 'poplin' was traditionally woven from cotton with a corded surface. The cloth is sometimes held to be the 'pope's cloth' because it is thought the word is derived via the French from the Italian, *papalino*, meaning papal. What is not disputed is that poplin was originally made in Avignon, in southern France, the papal residence from 1309 to 1378.

Pull the wool over someone's eyes

This expression meaning 'to deceive' comes from the days when wigs were the fashion. They were commonly known as 'wool' because of the resemblance to a sheep's fleece, especially wigs with tight curls. Therefore, to pull the wool over someone's eyes would be to stop them seeing what was happening around them.

Rosewater

One of the earliest perfumes known in England, rosewater has been used in a variety of ways for centuries either as an additive or in its own right. In the nineteenth century it took on a figurative use to describe any words or actions that were thought to be gentle, delicate or sentimental. In one of his works the novelist, William Thackery, uses the expression to good effect: 'Not dandy, poetical, rosewater thieves, but real downright scoundrels.'

Set your cap at someone

For 'cap' you can read hat or bonnet and one school of thought suggests that it relates to the wearing of beguiling or alluring headgear with a view to impressing a man. Certainly it means trying to win someone's favour; but another idea is that it has nothing to do with headgear at all but comes from a French nautical term, *mettre le cap sur*, meaning to head towards or steer for. Whatever its origin, the expression was in use in the early nineteenth century.

Sit on her skirts

As gentle as such an offence may sound, in the sixteenth century it was the expression used when you managed to revenge yourself against a woman. To 'sit on her skirts' was to 'pin her down' and give the object of your anger a severe punishment. Curiously, to 'sit on his coat tail' involved pinning a man down, but only in the financial sense. If a woman 'sat on a man's coat tail' she was dependent on him and his money.

Soul above buttons

We must all surely have heard someone referred to as having 'ideas above his station'. In Victorian times to have one's 'soul above buttons' was the reverse notion. Someone who was considered to have his 'soul above buttons' was someone who actually was, or was presumed to be, superior to the position he held.

Spencer

Like the cardigan, this is another item that took its name from the person who invented it. The second Earl Spencer (an ancestor of the late Diana, Princess of Wales) made a bet in the late eighteenth century that he could set a new fashion. He took to wearing a short double-breasted overcoat and soon won his bet. Several years later the name was applied to a short bodice-length jacket worn by women and children. Later still it was the name given to the knitted woollen or cotton undergarment that was the forerunner of the vest.

Stand upon one's pantables

The word 'pantables' is a corrupted version of another word that was known in the seventeenth century, 'pantofle', which was a high-heeled cork-soled shoe. It comes from the Italian word for slipper, *pantofola*. To 'stand upon one's pantables' was to stand on one's dignity, the allusion being to the height gained from wearing such slippers.

Strait-laced

For the origins of this description of someone who has more than his share of moral rectitude and a fair degree of prudery, you need to think of women's corsets or stays.

They were introduced into England by the Normans and remained in fashion until the twentieth century in one form or another. In the eighteenth century, corsets were particularly tightly laced to achieve the required tiny waist that was deemed highly desirable. It is this lacing that gave rise to someone being described figuratively as 'strait laced'.

Stretch your arm no further than your sleeve will reach

This is really just another version of the more familiar 'cut your coat according to your cloth'. It advises that one should not spend more than one can afford and should live within one's means.

Talk through your hat

As common a saying in times gone by as now, people who 'talk through their hat' make wild or exaggerated statements that have little basis in truth. There is no evidence of when the saying came into being, but the twentieth-century version is claimed to be 'talk through one's fly buttons'.

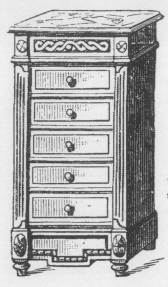

Tallboy

Originally a 'tallboy' was a long-stemmed glass, but we are more familiar with the name to describe what was essentially the wardrobe of the eighteenth century. The high double chests of drawers, stacked one on another, were made predominantly in mahogany – the favoured wood of eighteenth-century furniture makers. The smaller version, or 'lowboy', commonly had three long and two short drawers, but the tallboy boasted anything up to seven long drawers and two short.

To boot

Commonly used to mean 'as well as', 'in addition to' or 'moreover', the expression 'to boot' has nothing to do with footwear. It has been used for centuries and comes from the Old English word *bot*, meaning 'profit' or 'advantage'.

To trail one's coat

This was a way, in times long past, when you could literally 'ask for trouble'. The custom was that a man who was feeling quarrelsome or aggressive trailed his coat along on the ground, as a way of asking someone to step on it and thus instigate a fight.

Under petticoat government

An unflattering position for a man to be in, it was said of a man who was under the control or influence of his wife or any other dominant woman in his household. But while in modern times we think of a 'petticoat' as a quintessentially feminine article of clothing, it began life in Old French as *pety cote*, which means 'little coat' – and it was worn by men. In fifteenth-century England a 'petticoat' was worn under the doublet, or in the case of a knight, under his coat of mail. The name was later given to a female garment, again a type of small coat. Then somehow over the next hundred years the 'petticoat' slipped down below the waist and became a skirt worn exclusively by women. The name was given to an outer garment and also an undergarment (usually made of an inferior material) and it was not until the nineteenth century that the underskirt won the name exclusively.

Wear a hempen cravat

Fashionable though 'cravats' or neckcloths were for more than two hundred years, no one wanted to wear the 'hempen' variety, as it was a term for the hangman's rope. Therefore, 'to wear a hempen cravat' was to be hanged. The word 'cravat', however, is a corruption of *Crabat* or *Croat* taken from the Croat soldiers who served in the French Army during the Thirty Years' War from 1618–48. Depending on their rank, the Croats wore linen, muslin or silk scarves around their necks that were tied loosely at the front. The French set up a regiment, based on the Croat model, which was called 'The Royal Cravat' and part of the uniform was a linen neckcloth. The fashion spread to England where it held sway until the end of the nineteenth century.

Wear the breeches

Breeches were the most common garment worn by men from the sixteenth century to the nineteenth century, when trousers finally won the day. (Trousers had been worn from about 1730 onwards by soldiers, sailors and the lower classes but breeches were acceptable wear no matter what a man's status.) However, 'she wears the breeches' was said of a woman who usurped her husband's position and prerogative. Perhaps not surprisingly, many of the European countries had exactly the same expression. What is more, a woman who 'rules the roost' in Britain is still said to 'wear the trousers'.

Wardrobe

Originally the department in a royal or noble household responsible for the care and maintenance of wearing apparel, the 'wardrobe' then became the name for the room where clothes were kept. Such a room was usually next to the sleeping chamber and served as a dressing room. It was not until the eighteenth century that the name was applied principally to the large piece of furniture we know today, which in itself was a development of the cupboards and chests where clothes were traditionally stored.

Wide will wear, tight will tear

Just as it is generally accepted that if clothing is too tight it is more prone to tearing, this proverb was said to encourage good measure in government. It was said that if a man's actions were too tightly fettered it would lead to disorder. More moderate restrictions, on the other hand, stood a much better chance of being accepted.

When the weather is fair of your cloak take care

The advice contained in this expression is that you should be prepared for what might happen in the future. It is believed to come from a French expression, which, when translated, reads: 'When the weather is fine, take your cloak; when it rains, do as you will.' No one needs to be warned about obvious dangers, but it is sensible to look ahead and be prepared for dangers not apparently at hand.

Where the shoe pinches

We perhaps know this expression as 'there's the rub', as it means the root cause of any problem. The full saying is 'no one knows where the shoe pinches but the wearer' and it is believed to come directly from the reply of a Roman sage when asked why he was divorcing his beautiful wife. It is said that in response he pulled the shoe from his foot and having gained the questioner's agreement that it was indeed a fine shoe, then asked him to point out where it pinched.

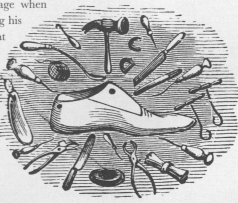

Upstairs and Downstairs

The great social divisions that have fuelled English history have been every bit as crucial to the development of the Englishman's home as the fabric of the building itself.

In our egalitarian age, with its modern machinery and services, even the most luxurious of homes can run efficiently without recourse to an army of servants to wash, clean and cook. But such ease is a post-war phenomenon and common speech still resonates with the divisions and traditions of our past. Many sayings we use today are rooted in the hierarchy of the English class system and the style of households such a hierarchy engendered. Other expressions also draw on the structure of the house to provide figurative food for the menu of metaphors and proverbs we enjoy. Rich fare it is indeed. Indeed, the very term 'upstairs, downstairs' is shorthand for the divide between the rulers and the ruled, the employers and the employed – and has been for hundreds of years.

Certainly, our language would be less intriguing without the contributions that have been derived from everyday domestic life.

All curtains and kippers

The origin of this delightful expression is unknown, but one feels that the actual items were chosen for their alliterative value as much as the expense involved in buying them. However, the expression is used of a household where appearances are put ahead of the actual standard of living enjoyed within.

All mops and brooms

While it sounds like a description of an untidy scullery, this Victorian phrase was used to describe someone who was drunk. The inference is, that like a mop or a broom, when you are heavily intoxicated you cannot stand up unaided. A similar expression for someone who was drunk was 'all keyholed', perhaps because someone who is 'worse for wear' has trouble getting his key into the lock.

An empty garret

When you know that 'garret' was a slang term for 'head', it is easy to understand that someone who had 'an empty garret' was one considered to be stupid or brainless. 'To have rats in the attic', on the other hand, was said of someone considered to be a harmless lunatic.

An Englishman's home is his castle

A saying dear to the heart of every Englishman, it was Sir Edward Coke, the Lord Chief Justice from 1613–17, who enshrined the principle in his *Institutes*, which are considered to be a legal classic. Coke was seen as a great defender of the common law against the right of the Crown and wrote:

> *The house of every man is to him as his castle and fortresse, as well as for his defence against injury and violence, as for his repose.*

The reference was to the fact that a bailiff should not have, and still does not have, the right to break into a man's home. But in modern times, an Englishman's 'castle' is not quite as inviolable as Coke envisaged it. Nowadays, under certain conditions, a number of public authorities have the right of entry to a private house – and in extreme cases can even destroy it, under the terms of certain compulsory purchase orders.

Backstairs influence

The term means to have an influence that is not publicly acknowledged on something or someone. It comes from the days when anyone seeking private consultation with the monarch, or a person of high office, would seek to use the secondary staircase, rather than that designed for state visitors. To win favour via the 'backstairs' equates in many ways to the more modern expression, 'through the back door', meaning an advantage gained without having to go through the normal channels.

Blowing away the cobwebs

These days, when you are in need of fresh air and a clear mind, you might well say that you need 'to blow the cobwebs away' and head out for a brisk walk. The allusion, of course, is to the cleaning the house of cobwebs that accumulate over time. In the seventeenth century anything that was regarded as flimsy or transparent in the way of one's actions, would be dubbed 'a cobweb'. A spider's web is so called because a Middle English word for spider was a *cob* or a *cop* and *web* is the Old English word for 'woven fabric'. What's more, cobwebs were held to have curative properties. A thick cobweb was said to be excellent at stopping bleeding, and when ague was a common illness, cobwebs would be rolled into balls and swallowed to obtain relief. In Herefordshire it was held that spiders did not like to spin their webs on Irish wood. It is claimed that the timber for Goodrich Castle, a former stronghold near Ross-on-Wye, was imported from Ireland especially 'to avoid the annoyance of cobwebs'.

Burning the candle at both ends

This is said of someone who exhausts his energies by getting up early and staying up late or is wantonly extravagant. While it is not possible to light modern candles at both ends, the expression dates from the time when it was. Tallow candles, the common light of the common man, were made from animal fat and often had rush wicks protruding from either end. Such candles were held in a pincer-like stand or bracket that allowed either end of the candle to be lit. To light both ends simultaneously was considered to be extravagant in the extreme and someone who did so would be accused of being 'a candle-waster'.

Carpet knight

In the sixteenth century, when this expression first appears, it was used to describe a soldier who preferred his engagements to be in a lady's boudoir rather than on a battlefield. In the nineteenth century the name was applied contemptuously to any soldier who stayed at home. It is suggested that it stems from the days when a man was knighted on the carpet before the throne instead of, as was more common, on the battlefield.

Charwoman

One only needs to know that a 'char' or 'chare' is an odd job, particularly that performed in the house, to understand the role of a charwoman. Such a servant was distinct from the household staff, in that by custom she was employed by the day to perform various household chores. In the late nineteenth century, such persons were also sometimes jocularly called 'charladies'.

Chauffeur

The fact that the person paid to drive a private vehicle is still called by his original French title preserves a little bit of motoring history. A *chauffeur*, in Old French, was someone who 'made heat' i.e. a stoker; and as the first motor vehicles ran on a steam-operated principle they needed to be heated up prior to being used. The 'chauffeur' was the man employed for the job, and while the development of the engine has made his job obsolete, his title lives on.

Creaking doors hang the longest

Sometimes said to cheer up the ill or infirm, the expression is meant to imply that those with complaints and frailties often outlive those who are seemingly more healthy and robust. The uncharitable connection is that the annoying sound that a creaking door makes may be likened to the moans and groans that some people who are indisposed are wont to make. Since the expression first came into common use in the late eighteenth century, the word 'doors' has sometimes been replaced by 'gates' – but the implication remains the same.

Daylight robbery

This is a term that is applied to an extortionate or excessive charge for something. The allusion is that the action is overtly carried out without any attempt to disguise or conceal it. There is a school of thought, however, that favours the explanation that the expression came about from the much-hated Window Tax that was first introduced in 1695 and lasted, in various revised forms, until it was finally abolished in 1851. During this period many homeowners blocked up windows to reduce their liability, and no doubt considered the Crown guilty of 'daylight robbery'. As enchanting an idea as this is, unfortunately it remains unsubstantiated. As an aside, there are still many people who confuse the windows blocked up to avoid payment of Window Tax with the false windows that were often incorporated into homes to maintain the exterior symmetry and proportions.

Dead as a door nail

The 'door nail' in question is the large-headed stud that is hit by the doorknocker. The assumption is that anything that takes such a hard and constant pounding must, indeed, be totally lifeless. Variations on the saying included, 'dead as a herring', 'dead as Julius Ceasar', and 'dead as a tent-peg' but the 'door-nail' has survived them all.

Doors

As you would imagine there are several English metaphors that feature the door, and the allusions are obvious. 'To slam the door in someone's face' is to stop someone from following his desired course of action; if something is discussed or happens 'behind closed doors' it is being kept deliberately secret or confidential; and 'to live up to the door' is to live to the full extent of your means. In Ireland there is a saying, 'Wide is the door of the little cottage', meaning that the needs of the poor are great.

Door-knob

Like so many English expressions, this one comes from rhyming slang. It was a word for a 'bob', in itself the common word for a shilling.

Doormat

Initially a slang term for a full beard, 'doormat' in the late nineteenth century turned into the colloquial name for the heavy moustache that had become the fashion of the day.

Doorstep

In the twentieth century when the noun is used as a verb, it becomes journalistic slang. 'To doorstep' someone is to call at his house without prior arrangement in the hope of obtaining an interview. More general use of the word is found in expressions such as 'on your doorstep', which is said of an event or eventuality that is closer than you might imagine it to be, and, of course, 'a doorstep', is also a thick slice of bread.

Eavesdropper

If guttering had been invented in the fifth century, the name for someone who listens secretly to other people's private conversations might be completely different. As it was, under Saxon law, homeowners were obliged to leave a space around their property for the water that ran off the eaves. Such a space was known as an *yfes drype*, eaves-drip or eaves-drop. Anyone who placed himself inside that space to hear what was going on in the house, consequently became known as an 'eavesdropper'.

Elbow grease

The perspiration caused by hard manual labour was known, in the seventeenth century, in a derisory way, as 'elbow grease'. In time, the term was applied to the energy needed to undertake such tasks as might generate the sweat in the first place. Whether knowingly or unknowingly, that change echoed the thinking of the early Greeks, who considered sweat to be the essence of strength and vigour. The reasoning was that if a man exerted himself to the extent that he sweated, he was sapped of energy and drained. Therefore, the fluid itself must be an essential part of physical power. There are tales of soldiers spreading the sweat of their horses onto their own bodies to improve their strength; and it was not unheard of for men to drink the sweat of famous warriors in the conviction that it contained courage. When we wish someone 'all power to your elbow', if they are undertaking a seemingly difficult task, we may not know it, but we are harking back to the earliest Greek physiology. The potency of 'elbow grease', still considered to be 'the best furniture oil', remains undiminished.

Hang up one's hat

It was customary for visitors to a house to hold their hats in their hands or to wait until it was taken and hung up by a servant. To 'hang up one's hat' by oneself was seen as a sign that someone felt at home and the expression came to mean just that. It was also used ironically to suggest that a person might be taking liberties in making himself too comfortable in another man's house.

Hinge on something

We all know that when someone says something 'hinges' upon something else, that the 'hinge' is the deciding factor and the allusion is to that essential mechanism that means a door can open and shut. Hinges also appear in several other expressions and all echo a similar sentiment. 'Big doors swing on small hinges', implies that major events can be determined by seemingly small matters. Someone with 'no hinge to his back', is someone who is independent and not bound to anyone – whereas someone who is 'off his hinges' is out of sorts or ill. To be 'unhinged', however, has a stronger meaning and is used to describe someone who is demented or crazed.

Home sweet home

An American playwright and lyricist was responsible for this often-quoted catchphrase. In 1822 John Howard Payne wrote his most successful musical drama, *Clari, the Maid of Milan*. Included in the operetta was a song entitled *Home Sweet Home*, an excerpt of which runs:

> *Mid pleasures and palaces though we may roam,*
> *Be it ever so humble, there's no place like home;*
> *A charm from the skies seems to hallow us there,*
> *Which, seek through the world, is ne'er met with elsewhere.*
> *Home, home, sweet, sweet home!*
> *There's no place like home! There's no place like home!*

The song became the great hit of its day and was much performed thereafter.

Hoover up

The efficacy of the first domestic 'beats as it sweeps as it cleans' vacuum cleaner is reflected when someone 'hoovers up' his food. The expression is used of someone with a healthy appetite who may not always remember his table manners. In a literal sense, the name of the first American manufacturer of what was a household revolution, has become the generic noun and the verb relating to the machinery, as well as to the task of vacuum cleaning. William H. Hoover owned an ailing harness and saddle business when he saw the potential and bought the rights to an invention patented by one of his relatives, a Mr James Spangler. According to Christina Hardyment, in her book for the National Trust, *Behind the Scenes*, this 'asthmatic school janitor in Ohio … He attached one of his wife's pillowcases on to a broomhandle to catch the dust drawn up by a fan driven by a small electric motor.' It should be stated, however, that at the same time as Mr Spangler was busy inventing his cleaner, a similar, although much weightier, industrial machine had already been patented in England by Hubert Cecil Booth, a fairground designer. In the end, it was the Hoover Company that realised the full potential of the domestic market, and the rest, as is commonly said, is history.

House-dove

This gentle description was used in the sixteenth century to describe someone who preferred to stay at home, rather than venture out into the social whirl.

Housemaid's knee

The medical condition, bursitis, is an acute inflammation of the *bursa*, which is one of many round, flattened sacs in the body that separate bare areas of bone from overlapping muscles or skin and tendons. Inflammation of the knee bursa, which is between the patella and the skin, is commonly known as 'housemaid's knee'. The complaint is so called because anyone who spends a lot of time kneeling on hard floors is prone to it; and many a housemaid suffered from the condition having spent hours scrubbing and polishing floors. It is also sometimes referred to as 'vicar's knee' and was considered an occupational hazard of the clergy and nuns alike.

Housewarming

Quite when a party held by the new owners of a house to celebrate their arrival came to be called a 'housewarming' is unknown but reflects, perhaps, the glow of good cheer that is common to such occasions. An ideal present to take to a 'housewarming' might be a houseleek, the common name for *Sempervivum*, a family of evergreen plants with rosettes of oval or strap-shaped pointed leaves. Traditionally, houseleeks were considered to be a protection against fire – a real housewarming – and there are several superstitious beliefs connected to the plant. It was also assumed that as houseleeks offered protection against fire, they would also help heal the effects of it. Consequently, the leaves were used as First Aid for all manner of household scalds and burns.

Join the household brigade

When the threat of war was on everyone's mind and the various regiments were actively recruiting new men, this expression took hold. It meant, quite simply, to get married.

Jump over the besom (or broomstick)

There are various forms and meanings to a besom, or broomstick, wedding, which has traditionally been associated with gypsies. In the Romany ceremony, a broom was laid on the ground and the couple jumped backwards and forwards over it, holding hands as they did so. This ceremony gave rise to 'jumping over the broomstick' meaning to marry or wed informally. However, in other circles, to 'jump the besom' meant to ignore the marriage ceremony all together, and live together as man and wife. In Yorkshire and in Lowland Scots a 'besom' was a derogatory word for a woman but, elsewhere in Yorkshire, to say that a woman had 'jumped over the besom' was to say she had an illegitimate child.

Keep a good house

This phrase has nothing to do with the cleanliness or order of a home, but was simply advice to provide wholesome and plentiful meals.

Keep the heps before your mouth

A 'hep' is a dialect word for a hasp or a door-latch and to 'keep the heps before your mouth' meant keep quiet and say nothing. In the north of the country the dialect word for a 'hep' was a 'sneck', and to be 'as common as a sneck' was to be very common indeed.

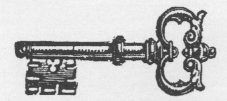

Key of the house

In the seventeenth century it was understood that the 'key' of any house was its mistress. Be in favour with the wife and you will always be assured of a welcome.

It was also common to say that 'the used key is always bright', meaning that an active mind will not rust away. At the same time, no one would be anxious to 'leave the key under the door', as it was a slang term for going bankrupt.

Kicked upstairs

This expression is indeed rooted in the house – but not the domestic one. The phrase is usually associated with politics and the elevation of someone from the House of Commons to the House of Lords. The insinuation is that although ostensibly being given a promotion, the person concerned is being removed from a more responsible and active position to one less influential. Despite the modern sound of the expression, it was known and used in the seventeenth century by Lord Halifax, then Chancellor of the Exchequer.

Make a clean sweep

To 'make a clean sweep' is to start something afresh and begin all over again. In times past, however, the simple chore of sweeping needed much consideration. It was believed that dust should always be swept inwards, as to do otherwise was to incur bad luck. To sweep dust out of a door was to risk losing the family fortune, and to carry dust downstairs after midday suggested that a corpse would soon be carried down the same stairs. For the same reason, it was ill-advised to use a besom made of birch-twigs or green broom in May.

Meet on the stairs and you won't meet in heaven

This is just one of the many superstitions surrounding the humble staircase and underlines the concerns people held about passing someone else on the stairs. Such a meeting was to be avoided at all costs and the onus was on the person at the top of the stairs to wait until the person going up or going down had reached his destination. If this was not possible, the two people concerned needed to cross their fingers as they passed, in the hope of avoiding pending misfortune.

Monkey up the chimney

If a householder had 'a monkey up the chimney' he had a mortgage. 'Monkey' was, and still is, a slang term for five hundred pounds. The alternative expression for a mortgage was, to have 'a monkey with a long tail'.

Narrow house

While it could be a description of a tenement, a 'narrow house' was a euphemism for the grave. Another popular term for the same thing was a 'long home'.

New brooms sweep clean

The efficacy of a new brush or broom has been appreciated by many a housewife and maid for centuries but a 'new broom' in this expression relates to a person newly appointed to a position who is zealous in making changes to staffing and procedures. In 1546 Heywood's *Dialogue of Proverbs* lists the expression as 'the grene new brome sweepeth cleane' and suggests the meaning then was as it is today. The Irish add an extra dimension to the expression when they say, 'A new broom sweeps clean, but the old brush knows the corners.' That is to say that an experienced person is better equipped to deal with the intricacies of the situation.

Nook-shotten

A nook is a small out-of-the-way corner and the term 'nook-shotten' was common in Cheshire to describe something that had been put into just such a place and forgotten.

When used to describe a person, the implication was that he or she was neglected.

Not worth a rush

Long before carpets were invented, rushes were strewn to provide floor covering. In medieval homes, the rushes were renewed or replaced if an important guest was expected. Someone who was not considered worthy of such an honour would have to put up with used rushes or none at all. Figuratively the expression came to be used to describe something or someone considered worthless.

Paraphernalia

For the true meaning of 'paraphernalia' you need to turn to law. The term was applied to the personal articles that a woman was allowed to keep and treat as her own even after she got married. As the goods in question were often jewellery and accessories, the word came to stand for a collection of any personal belongings. In Scotland the word became 'parafinelly' or 'parafin' and was a slang term for fussy or over-elaborate clothes.

Pin money

The provision made for a wife's personal expenditure is called 'pin money' and dates back to the Middle Ages when pins were expensive items, but much used to fasten clothes, and so an allowance was made for the purpose. The earliest known pins were sharpened fish bones or splinters of bone or thorn. Later pins were made of iron or bronze wire, and later still brass. The expense of a pin was in its manufacture. It took eighteen people, each performing a different task, to make a single pin and it wasn't until the mid-nineteenth century that pins were mass-produced cheaply. The original meaning of the term 'pin money' waned as the fashion for other fastenings waxed, and while a woman could then spend her 'pin money' on other things, the expression lived on.

Queen Anne front and Mary Ann back

One of the problems of the late seventeenth and early eighteenth centuries was how to combine, in domestic architecture, the desired dignity and expansiveness of the Classical with the desire for comfort and a home of a manageable size. The so-called 'Queen Anne' house was the perfect solution. The name comes from the great popularity of the style during Anne's reign, although the key elements of the design were already established before she came to the throne in 1702, and were essentially Dutch in origin. In the north of England the expression 'Queen Anne front and Mary Ann back' was used to describe something that had the outward appearance of being grand and high-class, but was, in reality, ordinary or commonplace.

Rain stair rods

You will have experienced 'stair rods' rain, even if you were not aware that that is what it can be called. Very heavy rain that falls in seemingly vertical lines was so called in reference to the metal or wooden rods that were commonly used to secure a stair carpet in the bend of each step. Modern carpet-grippers, which are fixed under the carpet, have made the use of stair rods a rarity.

Snow on the roof

The full saying is 'There may be snow on the roof, but there's fire in the furnace'. It was a polite way of explaining that although a man might be advanced in years he was not too old to show an interest in women.

Stairs without a landing

Prisoners in the nineteenth century would be well aware of what 'stairs without a landing' were. It was the colloquial name for the treadmill that was much favoured by prison reformers of the time. It was a large cylindrical wheel driven by the weight of the prisoners treading steps on its exterior, the resistance provided by large vanes in the air. In a few prisons such treadmills were used to grind corn or pump water, but generally the labour itself was considered to be the value and the power generated was not utilised.

Stitch in time

One of the most familiar of all English proverbs, 'a stitch in time saves nine' is used to suggest that prompt action now will save undue work in the future. There have been various sermons and treatises applauding the wisdom of the saying, including one by a Noah Webster, who in his work *The prompter; or Common Sayings, and subjects, which are full of common sense*, published in 1808, is adamant that:

> ... *in no article does a 'stitch in time' save so much as in government. One public officer neglects his duty a little, another cheats a little, but these peccadilloes are*

overlooked; the mischief is not great …
until at last a thousand little evils
swell into a great public one.

Take it in snuff

The 'snuff' in this metaphor is not the powdered tobacco that became very fashionable during, and after, the Restoration (Queen Anne was even a devotee), but the 'snuff' of a candle, the burnt out and smoky end of the wick. 'To take it in snuff' meant to take offence or be in a huff.

Threshold

Literally the doorsill, there is some debate as to why the 'threshold' got its name. There are those who will tell you that the word comes from the Saxon, *thærsewald*, meaning door-wood; others fancy that it is so called because it stopped the straw, a residue of 'threshing' that was commonly strewn on the floor, from blowing away; the third view is that it also comes from the idea of 'threshing' or 'stamping', but is therefore something you 'tread on' to enter a house. Whatever the truth, the threshold was considered an important element of the house, in particular with regard to a new wife. To avoid the danger of tripping or stumbling over the threshold, and thus ensuring a marriage fraught with disaster, the bridegroom was obliged to carry his bride into her new home – a tradition upheld even today. In its figurative sense, threshold means the beginning or start of something. In the nineteenth century, the Sussex coast was referred to as the 'threshold of England'.

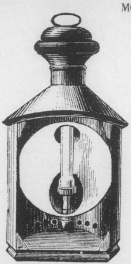

Trim one's lamps

To trim was a synonym for 'to thrash' and your 'lamps' were your eyes in street slang. Therefore to have your 'lamps trimmed' was to receive two black eyes. In its literal sense of course, it was a necessary function to ensure lamp wicks burnt efficiently.

Throw the house out the window

A popular expression from the sixteenth century onwards, the expression means to make a great noise or disturbance in the home. Someone who disturbed his neighbours in such a fashion was said to 'throw his house out of the window'.

Up to the knocker

Originally, someone of whom this was said was equipped to deal with the demands put upon him. The allusion is that someone tall enough to reach the doorknocker is mature enough to manage any given situation. Later it came to be a more general term to describe something or someone considered to be very well (as in healthy), fashionable or stylish. Another expression, 'to have a knocker', again an allusion to one's front door, was another expression for respectability.

Wallpaper

These days anything that is bland, particularly music, or in the background and passes unnoticed, is referred to as 'wallpaper', but the original wallpapers were anything but. The Chinese had been making and using wallpaper for hundreds of years before it became fashionable in England in the mid-seventeenth century. It was a popular and cheaper alternative to the more expensive conventional wall hangings such as tapestries, leather and silk but in 1712 a tax was imposed upon wallpaper that restricted its use to only those who were wealthy enough to afford it. The tax was repealed in 1861, following the invention of cylinder printing machines that made the mass-production of wallpaper a possibility and the use of wallpaper finally took off.

Waste a candle to find a flea

This rather quaint expression sums up very neatly the idea of spending time, energy and money looking for something that is not worth the expense.

Wendy house

The author J. M. Barrie is responsible for the name of the children's playhouse. It is said he named one of his characters 'Wendy' in honour of the daughter of the poet W. E. Henley. Henley used to refer to Barrie as 'Friend' but Henley's young daughter, unable to enunciate clearly, distorted the nomenclature to 'Fwendy-Wendy'. Margaret Henley died when she was just six, but Barrie borrowed 'Wendy' as the name for the Darling daughter in *Peter Pan*, who with her siblings was enlisted to rescue the Lost Boys. The name, applied to little girls' playhouses, has stuck ever since.

Wooden hill

Children in Victorian times were encouraged to 'climb the wooden hill to Bedfordshire'; the 'wooden hill' being the stairs and 'Bedfordshire' the land of Nod: the land of sleep so named after the land to which Cain was exiled after he had killed his brother Abel. It was Jonathan Swift who established the popular meaning of the phrase in English, when he used 'going into the land of Nod' as a euphemism for going to sleep.